I STARTED TO BE A MINISTER

From Fundamentalism to a Religion of Ethics

By the same author

The Mosaic Eschatological Prophet (1957;
    monograph based on author's Ph.D.
    dissertation, University of Chicago)
The Literary Origin of the Gospel of John (1974;
    sources and revision of the text in antiquity)
The Noah's Ark Nonsense (1978; expose of the
    claims that the Flood occurred and that
    Noah's ark exists)
The Historical Approach to the Bible (1982;
    survey of the history and nature of the main
    historical methods of understanding the
    Bible)

REI

REI (Religion and Ethics Institute, Inc.) is
an educational nonprofit organization devoted to
research in religion and ethics. Unlike many
religious institutions, it is not tied to the traditions
of the past, but searches for new knowledge and
new directions, provided they are consistent with
science and reason. Its purpose according to its
charter is "to promote the discovery and
distribution of sound historical and scientific
knowledge in the fields of religion and ethics." It
seeks an accurate understanding of the past and
present, but its primary concern is the
development of the future.

Membership in REI is open to all at
moderate cost.

Howard Merle Teeple

I STARTED TO BE A MINISTER

From Fundamentalism to a Religion of Ethics

HOWARD M. TEEPLE

REI

EVANSTON, ILLINOIS

Published by
REI
P. O. Box 5510
Evanston, IL 60204

Library of Congress Catalog Card Number
89-92368

ISBN 0-914384-03-1

Printed in the United States of America

TO

Eltruda Branchflower Teeple, my mother
Charles Sheridan Teeple, my father
Gladys Windedahl Teeple, my wife
Daniel H. Schultze, my professor of "Bible
        History" at   Willamette University
W. W. Herman Clark, my professor of "Records
        of the Life of Jesus" at Willamette
        University

Contents

PREFACE

This book combines an autobiography, a personal journey from Protestant fundamentalism to a religion based on truth and ethics, and an inside view of how biblical scholars work.

What should be the foundation of religion? What is really important? Worship? Doctrines? Spirituality? Ethics? Knowledge? Does it matter if the beliefs are true or not?

While in high school my religion was biblical fundamentalism, which I believed wholeheartedly. "Bible History," a course at Willamette University (Methodist), awakened me to the realization that some fundamentalist doctrines are erroneous. A second course, "Records of the Life of Jesus," aroused my intense curiosity about what Jesus actually said and did. After college I read all the library books on the subject I could find in Oregon, where I lived. Next, I earned a Ph.D. in Bible, early Judaism, and early Christianity at the University of Chicago, followed by teaching religion at Bexley Hall Seminary (Episcopal) and West Virginia Wesleyan College (Methodist). Experience later as a professional librarian increased my capacity to use research libraries. The curiosity about Jesus' life soon expanded to curiosity about the origin of Christianity in general and its beliefs. Throughout my career I continued to investigate the question of Christian beginnings. I was convinced that if Christianity stands for anything, it should stand for truth.

Disillusion with fundamentalism caused me to discard all religion for a few years. Introduction to the Unitarian denomination opened my eyes to the fact that religion is possible without traditional beliefs. This experience led to curiosity about another subject, namely, the nature of an ideal religion. What should a modern religion contain? This is the second question that has deeply concerned me during my lifetime.

Observation soon convinced me that ethics are of vital importance. Acceptance of theological beliefs does not necessarily produce moral lives, but the practice of ethical principles does. The misconduct of some religious people and the noble character of some nonreligious people I knew led to that conclusion.

While in college I was astonished to find that the truth in religion was not reaching the people. This situation was--and is--most shocking in respect to the Bible and early church traditions. Considering the authority given to those two features of Christianity, one would expect the churches to understand them more accurately than others do, but such is not the case. The most informed are historians and the leading seminaries and departments of religion in colleges and universities; churches do not sufficiently pass this information on to laymen. Facts and reason do not necessarily prevail in religion, I am sorry to say. Instead, beliefs that are aggressively promoted prevail.

After more than fifty years of research, the time has come to draw conclusions. Originally I planned to present them in one book, an autobiography. But I found that an account of Christian beginnings is much too large a subject to attach to the end of an autobiography, so it will be a separate book entitled *How Did Christianity Really Begin?*

The present book reports my research projects in biblical interpretation. Most laymen have little knowledge of how biblical scholars operate, and this book should give readers valuable insight into the historical methods used and the sincere motivation behind the research, even when it leads to unorthodox conclusions. The quest culminated in the founding of the Religion and Ethics Institute. Pursuit of our goals has given my wife Gladys and me some unusual experiences. The book includes a survey of our ancestors, for I wondered what kind of religion they believed in and if they had ever questioned it.

Since this book is written primarily for laymen and the public at large, a special effort has been made to write plainly, avoiding most technical terms. All too often, scholars write for other scholars, not for the public.

Many, many people have contributed to my intellectual growth, including parents, wife, professors, authors, and friends. Notable among institutions were many libraries, Methodist churches, Unitarian churches, Willamette University, West Virginia Wesleyan College, and the University of Chicago. Gladys, my wife, has been a marvelous inspiration and colleague during forty-two years of marriage. In addition to her, six readers criticized the first draft of the manuscript: Rolf Erickson, Paul Gehl, Richard Higginbotham, Patricia and Thomas Jobe, and Arnold Nelson. I deeply appreciate their work, for all, I believe, told me what they really thought--the best kind of friends a person can have! Special thanks to two other close friends: to Rita Djuricich for preparing the manuscript for printing, and to William Murphy for designing the book jacket.

Evanston

PROLOGUE

Professor Herman Clark wanted to empha- ᵛᶦᴰᴱ
size two points. First, study your textbook care- P.76
fully, but do not read commentaries or other books
which interpret the gospels or the life of Jesus. After you have finished the course, you will be free to
read whatever you wish, of course. The reason
that I am asking you not to read other books now is
that I want you to form your opinions on the basis
of the source material itself, the synoptic gospels,
and not on the basis of what other people say or
think.

"Second, each of you is at liberty to think
and believe whatever you want. You will be
graded on how well you study the text, not on
whether you agree with me, your church, or anyone else. I hope you will think for yourselves.

"Now I am going to ask each one of you, in
turn, to tell us what kind of person you think Jesus
was. At the end of this course I will ask you again,
and we will see what effect, if any, this course has
had on your concept of Jesus. Your answer now,
and your answer then, will have no bearing on your
grades.

"Jim, would you like to start?"

"I haven't thought very much about it. I
guess I believe what I was taught in Sunday
school. Jesus probably was divine and died to save

mankind from its sins. I really am not too sure, though, and that is why I am taking this course."

"Ruth, what do you think?"

"I think Jesus is the Son of God who came to earth to reveal God's will to us and to save our souls, and that he was crucified and rose from the dead. In general, I believe what my church teaches, although I am not sure that everything the Bible says about Jesus is true."

"Charles, what do you think?"

"I definitely believe that everything the Bible tells us about Jesus is true. The Bible is the Word of God, so it all has to be true. I believe that God sent his only begotten Son from heaven to save whoever believes in him, just as John 3:16 says. I believe in Jesus' virgin birth and resurrection."

"Do you believe in his ascension and second coming?"

"Sure."

"Dick, what do you think?"

"I know Chuck, and he's a fundamentalist. I don't agree with him. In fact, I think Jesus was human, just like the rest of us. I believe he was a prophet who taught the Golden Rule and the love of God and our neighbors."

"Barbara, what do you think?"

"I don't agree with anybody who has spoken so far. All those miracle stories: virgin birth, resurrection from the dead, ascension to heaven. It's all myth! I don't believe Jesus ever lived."

The astonished students uttered an "O-o-oh," followed by laughter.

"I can see," said Professor Clark, "that we have enough variety of opinion here to insure that we will have some lively discussions!"

He continued his questioning until all students had responded. Then he resumed his lecture.

"I want to tell you how Dr. Sharman produced your textbook, *Records of the Life of Jesus*. He was the son of American Methodist missionaries in China at the close of the nineteenth century. He became Honorary Lecturer in the Department of History at Yenching University in Peking. He compiled the textbook by using several Bibles and cutting the synoptic gospels into separate portions according to their subject matter. Then he arranged the portions into three columns, Matthew, Mark and Luke, in parallel so that if the same story occurs in two or three of these gospels, the different accounts are located side by side on the page for easy comparison. In the same way, he arranged the sayings and the gospel authors' descriptions. Material that occurs in only one of the synoptic gospels is printed accordingly in that gospel's column. You will notice that the Gospel of John is not included; the reason is that it is so different from the other three that only in a few places does its material parallel that in the others. This textbook was first published by Harper Brothers in 1917.

"This type of book is called a synopsis. Other biblical scholars have compiled synopses too,[1] but only Sharman has labeled the portions with letters of the alphabet to facilitate group discussion. Thus I might ask you, 'In Section 18 compare Portion C in all three gospels. How do they differ?'"

That is approximately the way the first session began in a two-semester course, "Records of the Life of Jesus," at Willamette University in Salem, Oregon, in September 1935. It was the best college course I ever took, the one that aroused my curiosity more than any other, the one that determined my career. It was the course that launched me on a lifelong quest to learn how much or how little in the canonical gospels is true, to learn what Jesus really said and did, to learn how Christianity began.

Near the end of my search I became curious about another matter. How religious were my ancestors? Did any of them question the Bible or traditional religious beliefs? Did any ever investigate the beginnings of Christianity? Before I could even try to answer such questions, I had to find out who my ancestors were.[2]

1

PATERNAL ANCESTORS

William Branchflower, my maternal grandfather, was the only grandparent I ever knew; the other three died before I was born, and my parents told me very little about them. I knew that the Branchflowers were from Ontario, Canada, and I think that I realized dimly that the family came from England. Like many other Teeples, including my father, I supposed that the Teeples, too, were from England. I conjectured that the name probably was "Steeple" originally and that someone later omitted the S. About twenty years ago I learned to my surprise that my father, as well as my mother, was born in Ontario and that the Teeple family did not migrate from England. The Teeples came from the Palatinate in Western Germany. The tradition that they came from Holland arose from the fact that after they left the Palatinate they embarked at Rotterdam when they sailed to England, and then went on to New York. They were Germans, not Dutch. The family name was Diebel.[3]

Starvation, sickness, homelessness, death! Such were the miserable conditions of the German people in the Palatinate district in the Rhine Valley during the Thirty Years War (1618-1648). German princes and various rulers fought against the power of the Holy Roman Empire. Animosity between Catholics and Protestants added fuel to the flames of political war. Marauding armies devastated the land, and many Germans fled to the Low Countries and England. By 1674 at least 186 Germans, mostly Lutherans, had settled in the Province of New York; none of them were Teeples.[4] They were not free from persecution there either, for the Lutherans and Quakers suffered severe religious intolerance from their Dutch Reformed neighbors during the harsh reign of Peter Stuyvesant (1647-1664), which ended when the English took New Netherland from the Dutch.

The Palatinate regained prosperity under the tolerant rule of the elector Charles Louis, a member of the Reformed Church. He offered generous incentives to Catholics and Protestants alike to re-populate and rebuild his land, and many accepted his offer.

After Queen Anne granted William Penn the Province of Pennsylvania in 1681, he invited oppressed religious sects in Germany and Holland to settle in his land. In response thirteen German and Dutch Mennonite families, led by Francis Daniel Pastorius and Johann Kelpius, sailed into the Delaware River in 1683 and founded Germantown. Contrary to popular view, these were not the first Germans to settle in America; as we have seen, there were already many in the Province of New York. No Teeples were in this sectarian migration either.

But the Palatinate was devastated again when Louis XIV of France tried to conquer it in 1688. At the instigation of his aggressive minister of war, Louvois, the king ordered the destruction of Palatinate cities and countryside to deprive the enemy of supplies. The war, which lasted ten years, developed into a war of France against Europe. The Palatinate especially was left destitute, and for several decades thousands of Germans moved out of it.

Joshua Kocherthal, a Lutheran pastor in Bavaria, wrote a pamphlet in 1706, inviting other Germans to join him in emigrating to America in 1708 or 1709. The English Board of Trade sent him with 53 others to New York in 1708, where the party founded Newburgh on the Hudson River. In response to his pamphlet, 14,000 Germans are reported to have moved in 1708 from the Palatinate to England with the expectation of emigrating to America with Queen Anne's assistance.

In 1709-1710 the "Great German Exodus" to America occurred. The main cause of the migration was economic. The emigrants expected to obtain fertile farm land, and the English Board of Trade expected them to provide England with naval supplies, including pitch from the pine forests of New York. The English also hoped that the settlers would be a buffer against the French in Canada and the Indians in the Province of New York. To qualify, the emigrants had to be certified by a Protestant clergyman, have partaken of a Protestant Lord's Supper, and had to swear allegiance to the queen of England. After they had repaid the queen by several years of labor, the settlers were to be given the land on which they had settled. The first group in this exodus consisted of at least 3,000 people who sailed in ten ships at the end of January, 1709. Before they left, John Trebecco preached to some of them in St.

Catherine's Church in London, comparing their migration to the Israelites' entrance into Canaan.

Expectation far exceeded realization. Packed in "like herring," 1700 died from sickness or starvation on shipboard or soon after landing. Subsequent shiploads met a similar fate. A typical Atlantic crossing then lasted three and a half months. Most migrants in the Great German Exodus settled in New York along the Mohawk River, but a few settled in New Jersey. Wresting a living from the wilderness along the Mohawk proved to be extremely difficult and hazardous, and more Germans died in that struggle. The Board of Trade, as well as the settlers, was disappointed, for the project failed to produce much of the anticipated naval supplies. Yet the German migrations continued!

When the last portion of New Jersey land was purchased from the Delaware Indians in 1832, Shawuskukhkung, an educated Delaware Indian, addressed the New Jersey State Legislature and remarked, "Not a drop of our blood have you shed in battle; not an acre of land have you taken but by our consent." On the same occasion Samuel L. Southard, a legislator from Somerset County, said, "It is a proud fact in the history of New Jersey that every foot of her soil has been obtained from the Indians by fair and voluntary purchase and transfer--a fact that no other State of the Union, not even the land which bears the name of Penn, can boast of."5

The first white owners of land in Somerset and Hunterdon Counties, New Jersey, were Scottish proprietors, beginning in 1681. The proprietors bought land from the Indians, divided it into tracts for resale, and promoted the sales in Scotland. A considerable number of Scots came to New Jersey and purchased tracts, but other customers--mainly Dutch and a few French Huguenots and German Lutherans from New York City and Staten Island--also bought land. A few early settlers came from Canada. These purchasers established farms in the valley of the Raritan River. Later some small towns arose; German Lutherans founded New Germantown (renamed Oldwick in 1918); Dutch and Germans established Pluckemin. In 1702 the proprietors surrendered their charter to Queen Anne, and East Jersey and West Jersey became one province.

Hans Georg Diebel was my great-great-great-great-grandfather. Born in Germany around 1675, he became known in America as George Teeple. In early America changes in the spelling of the names of immigrants occurred often. George and his wife (name unknown) emigrated from the Palatinate to the port of New York. She died soon after arrival, apparently without having given birth to any children. Historical accounts (none are source documents) that I have read agree that the date was around 1700, and they regard him as the first Teeple to settle in America. His brothers Johannes (name Americanized as John) and Wilhelm (William), accompanied by Wilhelm's wife (name unknown) and two children (Georg Lucas--known in New Jersey as Lucas--and Johannes), and perhaps their sister Margaretha (Margaret) also emigrated from the Palatinate to New York.[6] They probably came later than

George, for only he is reported as arriving around 1700, and Theodore Chambers reports that "Johannes Taeuble," whom Chambers regards as John Teeple, was in New York in 1710, at the age of 30, and that he was one of the Palatines of the Great German Exodus.7

In 1727 George purchased from Morris Cramer some land at Burnt Mills near Pluckemin in Somerset County, New Jersey. The legal description of his land was Tract 51 in Bedminster Township.8 George's brother William was a tailor and settled at Pluckemin. Where were these Teeples before 1727? Apparently there is no record. Some of the early European settlers in New York and New Jersey, including many Germans from the Palatinate, were redemptioners; that is, they obtained passage to America by agreeing to become indentured servants here for a number of years.9 A few migrants were able to avoid that condition by paying for their transportation. Perhaps the Teeples were redemptioners before 1727.

George had two sons, Christopher and John George, by his second wife. In 1739, when he was about 64, he married his third wife, Maria Barbara Seifferlie, a widow, according to the records of the Lutheran Church in New York City.10 His name and that of his son John appear in the list of subscribers to St. Paul's Lutheran Church at Pluckemin.11

Jurgen and Naomi Castner were also my great-great-great-great-grandparents. Jurgen (called Jeremiah or George in America) Kassener

(Americanized to Castner) came from the Palatinate, probably in the Great German Exodus. Chambers states that he probably was the George Castner who was apprenticed to Governor Hunter in New York in 1710 at thirteen years of age.[12] He was a member of the Lutheran Church in New York in 1721. Sometime in the 1720s he married a girl whose first name was Naomi. One of their children was Margaret. Today three Castner red sandstone tombstones stand, side by side, in the cemetery beside the Presbyterian Church in Pluckemin. The forenames are not legible because much of the lettering has flaked off.

John George (known as John) Teeple married Margaret Castner in 1756. John was a tavern keeper in Pluckemin.[13] The two brothers John and Christopher, were among the petitioners for the royal charter granted to the Zion Lutheran Church in New Germantown and St. Paul's Lutheran Church in Pluckemin by George III in 1767.[14] During the American Revolution John and Margaret moved to Bordentown in New Jersey. A gravestone in the churchyard of St. Paul's recorded that they died in 1813 within three hours of each other and were buried in the same grave.[15] The cemetery no longer exists.

My great-great-grandfather, Peter Teeple, son of John George and Margaret, was born in 1762 near Bordentown, just south of Trenton. In July 1777 the Council of Safety met at New Germantown and issued warrants to John and Peter Teeple and others to appear before the Council and subscribe to the oath of Allegiance to the United

States. John took the oath, but Peter (age 15) did not.16 Two of Peter's brothers, George and John, served in the Continental Army under George Washington. Soon after the Council of Safety issued its warrants, something happened which instantly made Peter a United Empire Loyalist (the Patriots' label for such people was "Tory"). He had a fine horse, which he kept hidden in a barn for fear that it might be confiscated for war purposes. His fears were justified, for one day when he was leading it out to water, some Patriot cavalrymen came along and seized it. He was so angry that he promptly walked all the way to New York City and joined the British cavalry.

He was in several battles, and once while scouting in Virginia, the horse on which he was riding was shot and killed. He was a good soldier, tall and of commanding presence, according to old accounts. He rose to the rank of lieutenant and was placed in command of a cavalry troop which was part of the corps known as the "New Jersey Volunteers." At the close of the war in 1783 his troop was disbanded at Halifax. At that time he was offered great inducements to return with the British troops and join His Majesty's Life Guards. He declined, and afterwards considered that decision as the great mistake of his life.17

Peter, along with a large number of other disbanded soldiers and refugees, settled in New Brunswick, Canada, where Loyalist settlements had been established at Waterborough on Grand Lake and at Saint John. He became the captain of a trading vessel shipping goods between Saint John and New York City. Peter met Lydia Mabee in Saint John and married her in 1785; she was only fourteen years old.

The Mabees introduced a different religious tradition into my ancestry. In the middle of the eighteenth century Simon Mabee, a Hollander, and his French wife, Marie Landrine, emigrated to America and settled near Sing Sing (now Ossining), New York. They were two of my great-great-great-great grandparents. He was a descendant of Lord Pierre Mabille de Neve, a Huguenot born in Anjou, France, who lived around 1550. Their son Frederick married Lavinia Pellum, an English Quaker; he, too, became a Quaker. They lived in Massachusetts and had three sons and four daughters. Their children, including Lydia, were raised as Quakers.

In the Revolution Frederick and Lavinia sided with the British. At the close of the war the new State of Massachusetts banished leading Loyalists, including "some sixty graduates of Harvard," it is said.[18] Lavinia and Frederick, too, were banished and their home confiscated. They fled to Saint John.

Those United Empire Loyalists who took up farming in New Brunswick found that making a living from the rocky soil was extremely difficult. Interested in finding a better way, Peter Secord, a Loyalist, accompanied an English fur trader, George Ramsay, on one of his annual furtrading expeditions to the Great Lakes. Secord was very favorably impressed with the abundance of game, the fertile soil, and nature of the country near Long Point, the narrow peninsula on the north shore of Lake Erie, in Upper Canada (now in Ontario). Returning to Saint John, he persuaded his cousin,

Frederick Mabee, and others to migrate with him to Turkey Point, just north of Long Point. Frederick took along his family, including two sons-in-law, John Stone and Peter Teeple.

The "Mabee party" of eighteen men, women, and children started out in the fall of 1792, wintered in Quebec, and reached Turkey Point the next year, traveling up the St. Lawrence River and along the shores of Lakes Ontario and Erie. The men rode horses and drove cattle along the shores; the women and children came in boats, going ashore at night to camp. Their food is reported to have consisted largely of cornmeal and milk from the cows, but surely wild game must have been included too.

Frederick Mabee built the first log cabin in Turkey Point. Soon many other Loyalists arrived. At first all were illegal "squatters" there, but in 1795 Governor Simcoe visited Turkey Point, with the result that the Crown apportioned the land to the new Loyalist settlers, and the settlement was officially named "Charlotteville." A year after his arrival, Frederick died of apoplexy and was buried in a walnut log coffin on a hill overlooking Turkey Point.[19]

Peter Teeple was the first Justice in Charlotteville, officially appointed January 1, 1800, by the first General Commission of the Peace at York (now Toronto). Thereafter he was called "Squire Teeple." He was also one of the original three commissioners appointed in 1800 to administer oaths to officers of the Government of Upper Canada. In 1803 Judge Peter Teeple fined Francis L. Walsh two shillings for swearing two "profaned oaths." Peter aquired a very large law library, even though he lived in the wilderness.

Peter and Lydia were constituent members of the Baptist congregation organized by Titus Finch in 1804 near Vittoria. In 1807 the land was purchased upon which to erect the church, and Peter became one of the two trustees. Thus my paternal ancestors abandoned their Lutheran and Quaker backgrounds and became Baptists because the Baptist church was the only church around.

Peter served in the British army again in the War of 1812. During that war his valuable flour mill was burned down by a party of American scouts. After the war he and his family moved to Centreville (near Ingersoll), settling on land granted by the British government.

Peter and Lydia had nine sons and four daughters; one of the sons was Luke, my great-grandfather. It was recorded that whenever Lydia lost her temper--which I infer was frequently--, she would repent and withdraw into seclusion, pace back and forth with clasped hands and murmur repeatedly, "Lord, have mercy! Lord, have mercy!" Peter was said to have been methodical, dignified, intelligent, and a strong advocate of temperance. When he was about 80 years of age, a quadroon, a fugitive slave from the United States, made a pen and ink portrait of him. Before the slave had escaped, his mistress had perceived that he had a talent for drawing and had procured for him some instruction in that art. Learning of the fugitive's talent, Pellum, Peter's son, brought him home one day and got him to draw on a flyleaf of a book a portrait of Peter holding Pellum's infant son on his lap. It was said that the portrait was a faithful like-ness, except that it makes Peter's chin too pointed.

Peter was buried in the cemetery beside the Baptist church about two miles south of Centreville (not the Baptist church at Vittoria). I have no evidence, but it seems probable that Lydia was buried in the same cemetery. Today the church is gone and the cemetery is only a field along No.2 Highway near Beachville, Ontario.

Luke Teeple, my great-grandfather, son of Peter and Lydia, was born in 1790. When the War of 1812 broke out, he was visiting an uncle in New Jersey. He was arrested and imprisoned along "with about a hundred other British sympathizers. These Loyalist political prisoners were sorely tempted to desert their first love and join the American forces. One by one they weakened until only fifteen remained, Luke being one of the faithful few. At the close of the war they were lib-erated, and the uncle, although a patriotic Ameri-can, gave Luke a present in token of admiration of his pluck and endurance."20 Luke returned to the Long Point Settlement and married Nancy Finch.

Titus Finch, one of my great-great-grand-parents, was a soldier in the British army. He came with his regiment from Britain to fight the American Revolutionaries. During the war he and a comrade became ill with fever and were nursed by the comrade's British wife. The comrade died, however, and Titus married the widow. He was very pious and never entered a battle without in-voking a divine blessing on himself and the British troops. After the war he sought work in rural Nova Scotia. There he joined a Baptist church, which ordained him because of his religious zeal. Like many preachers in pioneer settings, he had little education and no seminary training.

Titus and his wife (name unknown) settled near Vittoria in 1798. There were not many Baptists in the Long Point Settlement, but the zealous Titus was determined to remedy that dreadful situation! After organizing the Vittoria Baptist Church, he preached in it for more than a quarter of a century. The Finches had five sons and three daughters; one daughter was Nancy.

Luke and Nancy Teeple were members of the church of which Nancy's father was the pastor. They settled at Vittoria and bought a two-story frame house on the hillside below the Baptist cemetery. Luke built and operated a tannery on the flat ground below the house. He was also a tailor and shoemaker.

Nancy and Luke had seven sons and four daughters. One of the sons was Titus Ridley and another was Peter Latimer; both used their middle names instead of their forenames. This is the only time, to my knowledge, that any children in my family line were named after Protestant martyrs. The Protestant bishops Nicolas Ridley and Hugh Latimer were burned at the stake together in Oxford in 1555 by the Catholic queen, Mary I. I have seen the plaque in the pavement on Broad Street in Oxford which marks the spot. Nancy and Luke may have named two sons after the martyrs because of the influence of her zealous Baptist father.

Luke died in 1849, when he was only 59. In 1984 my wife Gladys and I located and photographed Luke's grave and that of his infant daughter, Mabro (spelled "Mabrow" on her tombstone), in the old section of the Vittoria Baptist Cemetery atop a hill.

Titus Ridley Teeple, my grandfather, married Thecla Tamsen Sovereen. Apparently the spelling of the Sovereen family name originally was Soverein in Germany. In America it was Sovereign at first, but later some of the family changed to Sovereen, a spelling that probably resulted from English-Canadian influence.

According to tradition, Frederick Soverein, a Protestant, emigrated from southern Germany to New Jersey in mid-eighteenth century. In New Jersey he married Lavinia Culver, an "American girl." Here the spelling of the family name became Sovereign. In the American Revolution they espoused the Loyalist cause, and in their old age moved to Norfolk County in Upper Canada. They had thirteen children. Lavinia and Frederick Sovereign were two of my great-great-great-great-grandparents. They were buried in Waterford.

Many of their family also moved to the Long Point Settlement soon after the Revolution, including their son Jacob ("Jake") and his wife (formerly Elizabeth Pickle) with their three children. Jacob built a log cabin in Charlotteville and soon turned his home into a tavern, where settlers gathered to drink "grog" and spin yarns before the fireplace.

Jacob and Elizabeth's oldest son, Frederick Sovereen, married Mary Jane Hutchinson and settled in the township of Middleton about the time of the War of 1812. He was known in the community as "Uncle Frederick" and she as "Aunt Jane." She was industrious, hospitable, and given to offhand speech. Once when the sermon had been very long and the "conference" exercises were about to begin, she stood up in church, arms akimbo. The pastor stopped the proceedings to ask her what was the matter. She replied, "Oh, I just stood up to rest my hips a bit." Her father, Captain William Hutchinson, another Loyalist, was known for his jolly disposition.

On his land "Uncle Frederick" laid out and founded the village of Fredericksburg. The name of the town was later changed to Delhi. He kept a tavern there for over thirty years. He also established a plug tobacco factory in the village, and donated the land for the local Baptist church. After retiring to his farm east of the village, he died in 1875 at the age of 89. Mary Jane died in 1868 when she was 76. One of their sons was William Louis.

William Louis Sovereen married Mary Ann Kitchen. These two great-grandparents of mine were two of the witnesses to the marriage of my Teeple grandparents. Their signatures as witnesses on the marriage license demonstrate that by their day some of the family, at least, had changed the spelling of the surname to Sovereen.

Mary Ann's father, Joseph Kitchen, came from Newton, New Jersey; he was too young to have been a United Empire Loyalist in the Revolution. The cause of his migration to Canada was most unusual. While he was living in New Jersey, a friend decided to move to the Long Point Settlement. As he was saying goodbye, the friend implored him to repent and become a Christian. Soon afterwards Joseph "experienced religion," and eager to tell his friend, he walked five hundred miles to Charlotteville. To his dismay, the friend did not believe that he was converted because his experience had been gradual. "Why, Joe," said the friend, "you don't know anything about religion! TRUE religion is jist like poppin' out of a tar barrel into the blazin' light of the noonday's sun!"[21] That reaction was such a jolt to Joseph that for many years he himself had doubts about his conversion. He remained around Long Point and became a deacon and pillar in the church at Vittoria, however. He married Miriam Barber in 1809, and they had twelve children, one of whom was Mary Ann. Joseph was noted for his upright character, independence of thought and action, and powerful physique. He died in 1868 at the age of 82, and Miriam was 84 when she died in 1875.

After their wedding William and Mary Ann Kitchen Sovereen settled at Fredericksburg. One of their six children was Thecla Tamsen ("Tamsie").

Titus Ridley Teeple married Tamsen. I have their marriage license, still in fair condition. It reads: "This certifies that Mr. Ridley Teeple of the Township of Middleton and County of Norfolk and Miss Tamsen Sovereen of the Township of Middleton, County of Norfolk and Province of Canada West, were lawfully married according to law, this 12th day of December 1858. [signed] L. W. Folger, Baptist Minister." Three witnesses also signed: J. H. Hutchinson and the bride's parents, William L. and Many Ann Sovereen. The minister added this note: "The above couple were married by right of licence, L. W. Folger, B.M." [Baptist Minister].

Tamsen and Ridley had six children, the youngest of whom was my father, Charles Sheridan, born in 1876. Grandmother had poor health and died in 1880 when she was 40. Soon Grandfather moved with his family to Deckerville (north of Port Huron), Michigan. He was a portrait photographer, and his oldest son, Ernest, chose the same career. With his horsedrawn portable studio (one of this type is in the Smithsonian Institution) Grandfather visited neighboring towns and took portraits. Thanks to Ridley's and Ernest's profession, I have a considerable number of early photographs of the family; some are tintypes. Grandfather wore a long, heavy beard and mustache; Grandmother's poor health is very evident in her photographs. Grandfather may have moved to Port Huron, for I have a faint recollection that my father mentioned his own boyhood there. In 1886 Grandfather married Ida Louise Holley, a widow.

The first Teeple to move to the Northwest was my father's venturesome brother William. He built a cabin in the forests near Marysville, Washington. After my father's death I found in a locked trunk in our attic Uncle Will's enthusiastic letter urging my father, who was fourteen at the time, to move to the West. "Charlie, my boy," wrote Will, "it's wonderful here in the West. There is good trout fishing in the stream nearby, and I can shoot deer through my cabin window. Charlie, my boy, you ought to move out here."

The rest of the Teeples apparently moved to Marysville in 1891. There both Grandfather and Uncle Ernie continued their photographic profession. They took many large photographs of pioneer life around Marysville and Everett, especially of farming and logging. The size of the cedar trees in those days is astonishing. In some photos the logs lying on the ground are higher than the men standing beside them. My father had a collection of their photographs mounted on cardboard; after his death I donated them to the historical society in Everett.

Grandfather Teeple died at the age of 71. His grave is in a country cemetery near Marysville. One of the few items I found in the locked trunk in our attic was a black leather-bound book given to my father. Inside the front cover his stepmother had written in black ink: "From--Father and Mother at father's death Dec. 2nd 1904." Written by Lewis C. Todd, the book bears the boastful title: *A Defence, Containing the Author's Renunciation of Universalism Explained and Enlarged; The Notices and Aspersions of Universalist Editors, Answered and Repelled; Arguments and Principles of Universalists, Examined and Exploded, and Religion and Revelation Vindicated, against Skepticism and Infidelity.* It was published in Erie, Pennsylvania, by 0. Spafford in 1834. Todd's book is typical of nineteenth-century Christian apologetics; the author was as prejudiced as the title is long! The book evidently belonged to Grandfather originally; it suggests that he may have been narrow-minded in his religious views. The book must not have meant much to my father. He never mentioned it, and he kept it in the attic, separated from our bookcase in the parlor. He did not take it with him when Mother and he were divorced. Apart from this book, he probably never even heard of Universalists and their beliefs!

2

MATERNAL ANCESTORS

The first Corbins to migrate to America came from Warwick, England, to Roxbury, Massachusetts in 1638. In 1654 Henry George Corbin, a draper and son of Thomas Corbin, sailed from Warwick to Maryland in the ship "Charity" and settled in Vermont. Whether I am descended from any of them I do not know.

The earliest Corbin ancestors that I can definitely trace are Joshua H. (1792-1868) and his wife Sarah S. (1794-1869). They were my great-great grandparents. Their son George Hughson Corbin (1818-1866) and his parents are buried in the Oriel Cemetery near Woodstock, Ontario. George married Lydia Weston Bedford, the widow of Daniel Bedford. Lydia and Daniel had had four children, and many years later the Bedford connection was responsible for my parents getting acquainted, as we shall see. After marrying George Corbin, Lydia bore six more children (two died young), one of whom was my grandmother, Sarah Elizabeth Corbin. These Corbins were farmers in East Oxford Township, near Woodstock, Ontario.

My other maternal great-grandparents, Stephen and Mary Ellen Parker Branchflower, married in 1826 and were farmers near Spilsby in

Lincolnshire, in eastern England. They had three children in Lincolnshire, but two died there. The third child died of smallpox on shipboard when the parents emigrated to Upper Canada in 1830. Ellen and Stephen bought a farm of 100 acres in North Norwich Township near Woodstock. They bought the farm from George Laudman, who had purchased it from the Crown in 1800. (There was no homesteading in Upper Canada; land was originally either granted by or purchased from the Crown).

Stephen and Ellen had seven sons born on the farm. All survived--maybe the climate was more healthful than England's. All seven sons acquired farms nearby. The third son was my grandfather William.

In 1863 William Branchflower married Sarah Elizabeth Corbin. He may have bought his 100-acre farm when he married; it was located in East Oxford Township, just north of his parent's farm. In 1952 my wife and I photographed the house in which my grandparents had lived and my mother was born. It was a small, unpainted frame house to which a lean-to had been added later. The house has been torn down since we saw it.

Grandmother and Grandfather Branchflower had three children who survived infancy: Sarah Ann, the oldest; William Stephen; Eltruda, my mother, the youngest. Two daughters, born later, soon died. Almira died of pneumonia, and Lydia Ellen was scalded to death in Chilliwack when she fell into a tub of boiling water that her mother was using to scrub the kitchen floor.

In 1879 my Branchflower grandparents moved with their children to British Columbia when my mother was two years old. My cousin Kenneth Branchflower was sure that "Grandpa knew where he was going" when he left Ontario; something or somebody must have lured him to purchase the land, even though it was thousands of miles away. Grandfather took with him a muzzle-loading long rifle which was an army rifle with its bayonet removed and its stock shortened to lighten its weight for use as a hunting rifle. It is smooth bored, and he once told me it would "shoot either shot or ball." I still have it, and an antique dealer told me that he would date it around 1850. My grandparents traveled by train to San Francisco and by ship to Vancouver, British Columbia, then inland to the Chilliwhack Valley. "Chilliwhack" was a Chinook Indian name; later the spelling was changed to "Chilliwack." The small valley was fertile and beautiful, nestled among mountains with the mighty Fraser River flowing through it. But the Fraser and its tributaries had the mean habit of flooding, and clouds of mosquitoes from the numerous rivers, lakes, and sloughs made life miserable for Indians, white settlers, and livestock alike. Later an expensive engineering project alleviated that condition by draining Sumas Lake and adjacent areas.

The valley was still in the pioneer stage. Its first store and post office opened at Sumas in 1864. Its first church was a Methodist church built along the Atchelitz River in 1869; the first school house arose in 1871 in Sumas. In 1875 the nucleus of a town began at Five Corners where five roads intersected (and still do). The town became known as Centreville and today is the city of Chilliwack.[22]

Chilliwack's origin is rather unusual. Although the Methodists outnumbered the Anglicans in the vicinity, the Right Reverend George Hills, Lord Bishop of the Anglican diocese of British Columbia, decided that the Established Church should have its own house of worship there. So he arranged for the purchase of an acre of land for it near Five Corners from a Methodist farmer. In the abandoned town of Fort Douglas at the head of Harrison Lake was St. Mark's Church, an Anglican building. The bishop had the church dismantled, transported by six Indian canoes to Chilliwhack Landing on the Fraser and then inland less than two kilometers to the new site, and reerected. He renamed it St. Thomas's Church. Next he proceeded to provide the church with a town. Around Five Corners a blacksmith shop and a public school were soon constructed, and McKeever's Hotel was moved up from the landing.

Grandfather purchased a large block of land which extended southward from Five Corners. On it he had a dairy farm where the Chilliwack Airport is now located, and he operated the general store at Five Corners. I am not sure whether he established the farm and the store, or whether they were already there. He employed Indians to help with the farm work; an Indian girl made the butter and took it to the landing, from which boats carried it to market. Many Indians and white settlers bought goods at the store, and with income from both farm and store, the Branchflowers prospered. They were active members of the Atchelitz Methodist Church, and Grandfather taught Sunday school there.

Grandmother Branchflower was a sensible, hardworking, ethical person who taught her children that "it's better to suffer wrong than to do wrong" and "two wrongs do not make one right." Grandfather, too, was industrious and very ethical and he was a successful entrepreneur. But he tended to trust others too much because he assumed that if they were Christians, they were good too. He trusted another pioneer in Chilliwack, Allen C. Wells, who was a member of the same Methodist church. I have the wedding announcement the Wells sent to my grandparents, inviting them to attend the wedding of their daughter Lillie, "At the Methodist Church, Chilliwhack, Tuesday, August 11, '85, at 11 A.M." According to reports I received, Mr. Wells took advantage of Grandfather in a property deal, causing him to lose his property in Chilliwack.

Embarrassed that he had made such a foolish mistake, Grandfather wanted to move away; possibly the mosquitoes and the Canada thistles on his farm were additional reasons. He was attracted to a remote area in the Polk County hills in Oregon, twelve miles north of Salem, southwest of Hopewell. There, for a small amount of money, he was able to buy several thousand acres. Because he owned so much land, some neighbors called him "the King of the Hills." The land, however, was rocky and generally unproductive, but Grandfather prospered from it anyway by putting it to the use for which it was best suited, namely, raising large flocks of goats and sheep.

In fairness to Polk County, let me hasten to say that most of it is good land, and today even the red soil of the hills produces excellent orchards. The

Willamette Valley as a whole is one of the world's great garden spots. My parents' valley farm was only four miles from the edge of my grandparents' farm, but what a difference! Our farm had fertile soil, telephone, and a good road in front with neighbors within sight.

But my grandparents' farm was so isolated! In the long rainy season the narrow ungraveled road, two miles long, which led in from the main road, became so deeply rutted that a horse and buggy could hardly traverse it. The red mud stains one's clothing and sticks to everything like glue. Mother told me how very difficult it was to ride her bicycle on that muddy road to get the mail from the mailbox on the main road. Once she remarked to me, "One of the reasons I wanted to get married was that I wanted to get out of those hills!"

The Branchflowers' move to Oregon occurred in 1896. Aunt Sarah did not move because she had married a Scotsman, Alexander ("Sandy") Munro, and they owned and lived on a farm at Cheam, near Chilliwack. Aunt Sarah was healthy, industrious, sensible, and Grandfather's favorite child. Eventually she had nine children, all older than I. I got to know my three youngest Munro cousins fairly well: Helen, Delia, and Douglas. All three were endowed with a great sense of humor. Uncle Sandy was especially jolly and a marvelous story-teller.

In Oregon my grandparents and their grown children Eltruda and William worked hard and saved. They lived in an unpainted cottage that they built. Soon Grandfather bought better land called Whitcomb Valley, which adjoined his farm and yielded good crops of grain and hay.

Grandmother's health faded fast, however, and in 1905 she died after nine years in the hills. I suspect that the rugged conditions there and the psychological shock resulting from the move were the underlying causes. I have her shoe buttonhook, distinctive penknife, and an alloy hairpin which Mother saved.

Around 1915 Grandfather married a divorcee, Harriet, whom he called "Hattie." For her he bought better land nearby, on a better road, and built a fine large house and farm buildings, all well painted. Again, his trusting nature was his undoing. She stripped him of much of his land and money and divorced him in 1922. No matter how much she mistreated him, he loved her still.

After the divorce Grandfather lived with my parents for four years and rented out what remained of the farm. My cousin Ken told me later that Grandfather was an expert woodsman, with skills he had learned from French Canadians in Ontario. Ken said that when Grandfather was 87 he visited Ken's parents and claimed that he could chop a log in two with an axe faster than Will and Ken together could saw it in two. So they held a contest, and Grandfather won.

I used to sit beside Grandfather's chair while he taught me Bible verses. When the Branchflowers lived in Chilliwack, they attended "camp meetings," old fashioned revival meetings, held annually at Camp Slough. Grandfather used to sing some of the hymns to me. I remember "The Old Ark's A-moverin'."

> Verse: The animals went in two by two,
>   The elephant and the kangaroo.

Chorus: The old ark's a-moverin', a-moverin',
        a-moverin'.
        The old ark's a-moverin', a-moverin'
        along.

Little did he and I realize that decades later I would
write a book [23] exposing the foolishness of efforts
to find "Noah's ark" on Mount Ararat, and
demonstrating the firm conclusion of historians
and biblical scholars that the Flood story is only a
story, a myth which began in ancient Sumer and
was adapted by different cultures, including the
Israelite.

When Grandfather came to live with us, he
brought with him a Model T Ford truck with solid
rubber tires on the rear wheels. Such hard tires
were illegal for use on highways because they tend
to break up the road's surface. Therefore we used
the truck only on our farm, and I learned to drive
by driving it around in our fields--no traffic haz-
ards! I soon learned that the quickest way to stop
the thing was to step on both the brake and reverse
pedals at the same time.

Even though he was in his late eighties,
Grandfather hoped to operate his farm once more.
He especially aspired to raise sheep again. When
he was ninety, he caught pneumonia and we took
him to the Salem Memorial Hospital. He always
feared that if he ever became a patient in a hospital, he would not come out alive. And that is the
way it turned out; after one week there, he died.
Grandfather and Grandmother are buried in the
churchyard cemetery near Hopewell, Oregon, atop
a hill.

A bit of a dispute occurred when his estate was settled. His will left $1,000 to each of his grandchildren, with the remainder of the estate divided equally among his three children. At first the three tried to agree on how to divide his farm, but that failed because of the uneven value of different portions of the land. So the heirs agreed to sell the farm and divide the funds.

While still living in Chilliwack, Uncle Will married May Mathieson, and they had one child, Max. When Will's parents moved to Oregon, May refused to go and leave her relatives, so Will divorced her. Will helped his father on the farm and at times worked for a neighbor, Mr. Dent. Uncle Will told me that once when he was "drilling" (that is, sowing grain with a drill) for him, Dent expressed surprise that the amount of seed he took out into the field was always the exact amount. Will told him his secret: as he neared completion, he simply opened up the drill more if it appeared that seed would be left over, or reduced the flow from the drill if it seemed that there would not be enough seed.

Uncle Will married Cora Mae Massey, who lived across the Willamette River in Marion County. At first they bought and lived on a farm which adjoined that of his parents. Aunt Cora, however, disliked the isolation and red clay of the hills as much as my mother did. So they sold that farm and bought one on the northwest edge of Newberg, Oregon, where they built a large house and a large red barn. They had one child, Kenneth, born in 1907. Ken and I were good friends and played together when the two families regularly had Thanksgiving dinner at my house and

Christmas dinner at his. Occasionally the two
families made the round trip of 44 miles to visit in
the spring or summer. Photography was Ken's
hobby, and during World War II he was an aerial
photographer in the U.S. Air Force. Afterwards he
was a photographer for the U.S. Army Engineers.
Much to his mother's displeasure, at the age of 37
he married a neighbor, Grace Wurst, a widow with
two daughters. He outlived Grace, but died of a
heart attack when he was 69.

The survey of my ancestors leaves me with
some strong impressions of them. They were generally industrious and progressive. They were ethical people. As far as I know, all were honest and
tried to "do what is right." None were criminals.

They were generally religious, but their religion was rational and sensible, rather than emotional. I suspect that zealous, pious Titus Finch
may have been an exception, however. All belonged to mainline Protestant denominations:
Lutheran, Friends (Quakers), Baptist, Methodist.
Joseph Kitchen, in particular, appears to have had
an intelligent approach to religion.

Apparently no ancestor ever questioned or investigated religion, as I have, however. But none
of them ever had access to the information that I
have had. And access to information does make a
difference. To shield young people from unorthodox information was a major reason, or even the
major reason, for establishing parochial schools
and fundamentalist "Christian schools."

3

PARENTS

Both Chinook Indians and white settlers purchased goods at the Branchflowers' general store in Chilliwack. Some Indians had difficulty in pronouncing even the short form of my mother's name, Trudie. One day, when Mother was five years old, an Indian, a regular customer, entered the store and looking down at her, asked, "How's little Choojie today?" Mother indignantly replied, "I'm not a little Choojie!" The Indian, with a twinkle in his eye, said, "Oh, great big Choojie!"

Mother told me that sometimes her parents drove by horses and surrey to Cultus Lake for a family Sunday picnic. A beautiful small lake nestled in the mountains, Cultus Lake is now a provincial park, still popular, still unspoiled. The Chinook Indians called it *cultus,* "bad," because sudden squalls made the lake dangerous for boating. Occasionally the Branchflowers visited Harrison Hot Springs, a little farther from home, today quite commercialized.

I know very little about my mother's girlhood. I have three photographs of her taken by professional portrait photographers in New Westminster. I judge her age in them to be about six, twelve, and sixteen. In another portrait, evidently taken after the family had moved to Oregon, she appears to be about twenty, a beautiful woman.

I also have her girlhood autograph album, red and gold, well worn. The price is still written in it: 35¢. It contains autograph rhymes characteristic of the time, bearing dates from 1888 to 1899. Most were written while she lived in Chilliwack, but two were written after the family moved to Oregon in 1896. Her brother-in-law, Alexander Munro, wrote this advice:

> Dear Trudie--
> Fruit is sweetest when 'tis ripest,
> Love and kisses soon grow cold.
> Young men's vows are lightly spoken.
> Look out, Trudie, don't get sold.

The autographs range from sublime to comic.

> The memory of good actions is the starlight of the soul.

> Forget me not, forget me never,
> Till yonder sun shall set forever.

> As sure as comes your wedding day,
> A broom to you I'll send.
> In sunshine use the brushy part,
> In storm the other end.

> Writing in albums is all stuff.
> I'll write my name and that's enough.

Mother was nineteen when she moved with her parents and brother Will to Oregon. Her parents immediately sent her to McMinnville College (now Linfield College) in McMinnville, Oregon, for one year, where she studied elocution, piano, and art (oil and watercolor painting and charcoal drawing). McMinnville College, founded in 1849, was still very small. I inherited a photograph which shows the whole faculty and student body in the spring of 1897. Six persons are faculty and the other 43, including my mother, are students. Oregon, like British Columbia and Washington, was just emerging from pioneer times. Mother was very talented in elocution, and I heard her give "readings" at social gatherings at church, the Grange, and especially the Spring Valley Community Club. Some were serious, some humorous; some were poetry, some prose; she memorized them all.

Mother's art training, unlike that today, consisted of copying pictures instead of painting directly from life. She never tried to sell her copies, of course, but they were well done, and several of her oil paintings always hung in our home. Her painting of four cats still attracts favorable comment. She enjoyed painting, but never had time to do any after she married. Several times she remarked to me, "I hope that someday I can move into town and have time to paint again." Although her last year and a half were spent in town, she did not have the leisure for painting. When I was young, I was so optimistic that I thought there would yet be time in the future for whatever people wanted to do. I used to say, "There's always tomorrow." Now I realize that for many people, tomorrow never comes!

Although Mother was unhappy with the isolated life in the hills in her youth, one factor there alleviated the isolation. A mile away, through the woods, lived a girl of her age who became a close friend. I knew her later as Mrs. Walling, a widow. Both women played the piano; both were refined and cultured. When I was young, Mrs. Walling's two children, Claude and Lorene, were my schoolmates and friends at Spring Valley School.

Although born in Ontario, Father's early boyhood was spent in Deckerville and probably Port Huron, Michigan. His badly worn *Second Reader*, which I possess, bears his name and the address "Deckerville"; this shows that the Teeple family was living there in Michigan by the time Father was in the second grade. He was fourteen when his father moved the family in 1891 to the vicinity of Marysville, Washington. After that move the Teeples bought woodland, cleared part of it, and with trimmed cedar logs for walls and cedar shakes for a roof, built a cabin. Father once told me that he had associated with a bad bunch of boys and that they had done "some sinful things we shouldn't have done." Just what those wicked deeds were he never said and I never asked. A sense of guilt over those deeds caused his conversion to Christianity at the age of sixteen.

Father attended the Methodist school, Puget Sound University (founded 1888), in Tacoma for two academic years, 1896-1898. He was a mem-

ber of the school's Orophilean Literary Society
and sang in its quartet at the "open meeting" in the
University Chapel on February 25, 1898. The
"Programme" lists three musical numbers, two
recitations, an oration ("Annexation of
Territory"), and a "Question Box" conducted by
three students. I have my father's notebook
recording notes from a course on the Bible that he
took at PSU; the content of the course evidently
was quite orthodox. Later Father filled many of
the blank pages left in the notebook by pasting in
newspaper and magazine clippings--mostly po-
etry--of a religious and/or moral nature. I am not
surprised to find there also some rules for playing
parlor games, which he loved to play at parties in
our home.

He received good grades at the university,
and evidently was well liked by the administration. I have in hand two excellent letters of recommendation for him, both dated March 17,
1897. One is written by the Registrar, Charles
W. Darrow, and the other by Crawford R.
Thoburn, Chancellor.

"My thoughts take me back to last Sunday
when we were seated in the carriage on our return, and then again on Monday under the Oak
Tree while we were enroute for the mail. That
was and always will be a precious moment when
you said 'Yes.'" Thus "Charles" wrote to
"Trudie" on July 13, 1902, after he had proposed
on July 6 and she had accepted on July 7.

Lydia Corbin, one of my maternal great-
grandmothers, had had a son, James, by her previous marriage to Daniel Bedford. Thus James

was distantly related to my mother. Later James married my father's sister Vestilla, "Aunt Tillie." This slight connection between the Branchflowers in Oregon and the Teeples in Washington must have been responsible for the two families becoming acquainted.

Vestilla Teeple Bedford, my Aunt Tillie, took Charlie along when she visited the Branchflowers at their hill farm in 1902. Her plan to make a match between Charles and Eltruda succeeded, as the extract from Father's letter reveals. The young couple agreed to marry a year later. Eltruda and her mother accepted an invitation to visit the Bedfords in the following fall or winter. In addition to the proposal, photography and playing croquet with family and friends were highlights of Tillie's and Charlie's visit. Father coached Mother on how to take pictures with his large box camera, which made photographs on glass plates, not film. Photography was the only hobby he ever had; he developed the plates and made the prints himself.

When Tillie and Charlie ended their visit, the Branchflowers drove them six miles to Spong's Landing, the riverboat landing at Lincoln on the Willamette River. From this landing local farmers shipped sacks of grain to market in either Salem or Portland. The landing was named for Captain Spong, who operated the boat regularly between Salem and Portland. Before the boat arrived, Eltruda and Charles walked along the riverbank and discussed their future. After reaching Salem, Vestilla and Charles took the train home to Marysville, Washington.

Father was employed in a logging and lumber company's general store in Marysville. After working late for several days to catch up on the work that had accumulated while he was away in Oregon, he began at 11:10 Saturday night to write to Mother. Finishing the letter the next night, he wrote an account of his activities that day, Sunday, that provides insight into life in a small western town at the turn of the century. It especially shows the close contacts maintained among relatives, a condition very different from that of my own youth. Only rarely did relatives visit us on the farm, and even rarer were our visits to them, tied down as we were to milking cows twice daily.

According to Father's letter to Mother, Sunday was a very busy day. From 10 to 11 A.M. he taught Sunday school at the Methodist church, followed by attendance of church services. There he "heard a good sermon on "Thou shalt have no other gods before me." At noon there was a fire in a hotel, but the fire was out before he reached the building. Next, he watered and fed the company's horses which hauled goods to and from the store. His brother "Ernie" (Ernest) and wife "Flo" (Florence) "took dinner" with his brother Will. Father took dinner at home with his father and step-mother. "A young man called to take my step-sister, Armena, for a walk as soon as dinner was completed, so I soon took my exit." Father's sister Linnie taught Sunday school on Sunday afternoons at Kellogg Marsh, three and a half miles from Marysville. But she went to Everett that day and had asked Father to teach in her place. So he "wheeled" out on his bicycle and found that attendance was good. Then he visited his sister Mary, who lived with her husband George Templeton at Kellogg Marsh. George was away in Marysville at the time. Next, back to Marysville where Father again cared for the horses. Then, going to the back of the store to the office where he roomed, he resumed his letter to Mother. Next came "supper," and then church again for "evening services."

On Wednesday, October 7, 1903, Eltruda and Charles were married in her parents' home by "John Parsons, Pastor First Methodist Episcopal Church, Salem, Oregon," according to the marriage certificate. Her brother Will and his future wife, Cora M. Massey, were the witnesses. Why wasn't the Hopewell minister chosen to conduct the ceremony? Salem was twelve miles distant, but the Hopewell country church was only four miles away. The reason probably was that both the Branchflowers and Teeples at the time were Methodists, while the Hopewell church belonged to the Church of the Brethren. Considering the remoteness of Salem, the Branchflowers may not have belonged to any church at the time.

The married life of Eltruda and Charles got off to a rough start. His sister Vestilla had told him, "Charlie, as soon as you are married, show her that you are boss and are going to stay boss." And he took her advice. Mother was a sensitive, gentle, loving person; dictatorial treatment was the last thing in the world that she needed. The marriage never recovered from the effects of Aunt Tillie's shameful advice.

The lumber company transferred Father to Tacoma, and the young couple lived there for nearly four years. At first they lived in one of the numerous identical, unpainted houses the company built for its employees. Later they lived in larger, painted houses. Mother worked in a dressmaking shop along with eight other employees and the owner. Father continued to work in a company store, serving as both bookkeeper and clerk.

Once the store's cash did not equal the amount in Father's accounts, and the company accused him of stealing the money. He professed his innocence, but offered to pay the company the missing amount anyway. Both the company and Mother regarded his offer as proof of his guilt, but he stoutly maintained that he had not taken the money and that he had made the offer as a gesture of loyalty to the company. Knowing my Father, I really believe he was blameless. As far back as I can recall, I never knew either parent to do anything dishonest.

While living in Tacoma, my parents attended two world fairs: the World's Fair in St. Louis in 1904, and the Lewis and Clark Exposition in Portland, Oregon, in 1905. While living on the farm later, they attended the World's Panama Pacific Exposition in San Francisco in 1915. I am surprised that they took those trips, for throughout their married lives they never traveled outside of Oregon again, except to visit relatives in 1925. I assume that the daily chore of milking the cows was mainly responsible.

Grandfather Branchflower had given his three children farm land in British Columbia.

Aunt Sarah and Uncle Sandy lived on theirs at Cheam, near Chilliwack. Uncle Will and Mother sold theirs, and each bought land in Oregon in the vicinity of their parents' farm. With the $10,000 she received from the sale of her land, Mother bought 100 acres, the northern portion of the B. Frank McLench farm in the valley, eight miles north of Salem on the Wallace Road in Polk County. From the same funds she built a complete set of very good farm buildings, painted them, and had $1,000 left with which she bought lots in West Salem. (The lots were a poor investment, for she had to sell them at a loss during the Great Depression, after paying taxes on them for twenty-five years. She had wanted to sell them earlier, but Father always objected). The woodshed was built first, and the couple lived in it until the other buildings were constructed--the house came last. That was the usual procedure in establishing a farmstead because the farm buildings were essential to get operations and income started.

Father reduced the cost of constructing the buildings by working alongside the carpenters, and by the time the seven buildings were up, he was a skilled carpenter. He carefully selected the woodwork throughout the house and had it stained and varnished. The paneling in the sliding doors between the dining room and the parlor was especially beautiful.

A joke in our family was related to the fact that we had a very large house with four bedrooms, but only three people in it. The joke was that when Father planned the house, Mother objected that we did not need such a big one. Father optimistically replied, "Trudie, you don't know how many children we may have--we may need the space." When I was born, my parents must have been disappointed, for they never had any more children. Anyway, we always had plenty of room for the relatives who occasionally visited us for one or two weeks at a time. In my youth I especially enjoyed the attic, lying on the floor and reading, listening to the patter of the rain on the shingles above my head.

Father planned the farmstead well. He was inexperienced in farming, but someone--probably Grandfather Branchflower--must have given him good advice. The arrangement of the buildings, fences, and gates was perfect, and the barn was the most efficient I have ever seen. The driveway in from the road was built up with earth and gravel so that it drained well in the rainy season. The house was set far back from the road to escape the dust from passing wagons and buggies. Later I spent so much time mowing that huge lawn that to this day I have a prejudice against large lawns.

My parents were moderately successful financially because they worked extremely hard and the farm had fertile soil and no mortgage. Father arose at five o'clock to milk the cows; Mother got up at six, but I usually did not roll out until 6:30-7:00 (yes, I was spoiled, but at least I worked hard throughout the day and evening). We did not finish chores until ten o'clock at night--later than any of our neighbors. While I was too young to work in the fields, Mother sometimes drove our team of three horses and operated the binder, while Father shocked the bundles of grain.

Our farm was as self-sufficient as a farm can be. It furnished all the wood for cooking and heating in our home: fir, ash, and oak. We cut our Douglas fir Christmas trees from our own woods. A pit in the river bottom supplied all the sand and gravel needed to gravel the driveway and to make concrete. The mild winter climate and the abundance of rain in the Northwest permits the growing of every kind of fruit except tropical. Father planted a tremendous family orchard. We had at least a dozen varieties of apples, four varieties of cherries, two of pears, and two of prunes. The Hungarian prune tree loaded its limbs each year until they broke with large, pear-shaped, utterly delicious fruit (really plums, not prunes). We had a quince and two English walnut trees. We had strawberries, raspberries, blackberries, loganberries, youngberries, boysenberries, gooseberries, and currants. The garden, three-fourths of an acre in size, overwhelmed our little family of three. In addition to all kinds of annual vegetables, we had rhubarb and asparagus. After the orchard was bearing, Mother annually canned, on a hot wood range, quarts and quarts of fruits and vegetables. How I loved her sweet green-tomato pickles, Bing and Lambert black cherry pies, and fresh peach cobblers. Sometimes she canned young beef that Father butchered; occasionally he butchered a hog. Mother made butter with a barrel churn, and sometimes Father made ice cream. I helped as soon as I was old enough, and enjoyed it. We worked like slaves, but feasted like kings!

We had such a surplus of food that we fed apples to horses, cows, and hogs. Father and I sliced by hand, with corn knives, hundreds of pumpkins, squash, and potatoes and put them in the cows' mangers. Our livestock loved the menu.

Because of the distance of the farm from town, Father repaired everything himself. As I grew up, I learned the skills from him. We did carpentry, plumbing, electrical wiring, painting, paperhanging, concrete mixing and laying, harness and machinery repairing, and overhaul of cars, trucks, and tractors. Later I learned machine shop work from a neighbor who had a shop on his farm. When I was in my twenties, our roofs began to leak and I reshingled them all with cedar shingles. When I was reshingling the cupola on the top of our high barn, I slipped and almost fell off the barn. One Sunday afternoon I began to repaper my bedroom, and when I had the first strip on the wall, my cousin Kenneth arrived with his parents for a visit. Ken took a close look at the paper and remarked, "I believe that paper is up-side-down!" With roses facing in several directions in the pattern, I had not noticed it, but Ken was right, so we pulled the paper off the wall and rehung it.

Father early constructed "the grade," a road connecting our level upland with the river bottom eighty feet below. The grade was so steep that our horses could hardly haul gravel up it. When I was four years old I climbed off the wagon, contrary to Father's orders, just before the horses found the strain too much for them and started to back down the hill. Horses, wagon, and gravel went over the edge of the road, landing up-side-down in the brush on the steep hillside.

Father built an ingenious cage for "breaking up" broody hens which wanted to hatch eggs instead of laying them. The cage was made of lath spaced about two inches apart, thus depriving the hens of a solid floor to sit on. It was mounted on a pipe which ran through the middle and suspended the cage in the air. As hens moved around in it, the cage revolved, further discouraging a brooding psychology. For good measure, our family would give it a good spin as we walked by.

Eventually Father cleared a one-acre field at the foot of the grade. One year he planted cantaloupes in the whole field, but we did not have time to harvest and sell them. My playmate Vernon Windsor and I sat down in the middle of the patch one day and ate until we were stuffed. Later Father cleared another acre and half and planted peach trees on the sandy end. Peaches, too, ripened at a busy time, so some were harvested and some were not. When I was in high school, a classmate drove out from Salem one Sunday and we amused ourselves by shooting peaches off the trees with my .22 caliber rifle.

The section of the river bottom that was the most fun was the fishing and picnic area, with its slough, woods, and large open area ideal for ball games. The river bottom used to flood in the spring. Before the federal government built flood control dams, Father constructed some ingenious portable picnic tables, benches, and two outhouses that were easily dismantled for storage in our machinery shed. When they were needed for large picnics, we hauled them down to the picnic grounds and set them up. Groups from our church had free use of the grounds, but we charged the Oregon Lumbermen's Association $50 per day for its annual picnics.

My parents lived at the time of the second great power revolution in farming. The first revolution, of course, was the shift from human power to ox, mule, and horse power, a change which occurred many centuries ago. The second revolution, from horse power to tractor power, occurred in our community in four decades, 1910-1950. I remember that when I was five to eight years old I sometimes walked beside my father, talking to him, when he was plowing with horses. Plowing with horses was very tedious work. How many times do you think you would have to walk across a forty-acre field to plow it, one sixteen-inch strip at a time? And it would add to the fun if you happened to plow up a yellow jackets' nest!

Early in the 1920s we acquired a Fordson tractor; the Fordson was the pioneer low-priced tractor just as Fords were the pioneer low-priced cars and trucks. The main problem with Fordsons was that they were hard to start. In cold weather we had to build a fire under the crankcase to warm up the oil to enable us to spin the crank fast enough to start the motor.

Horse farming versus tractor farming was a lively debate topic among farmers in the 1930s. The Great Depression fostered resistance to tractors because the farms produced the food for the horses, but for tractors one had to buy gasoline and oil. One of our neighbors, Joe Wilwert, born in Austria, added another argument for horses; like all livestock they fertilize the soil. He expressed it this way: "When you stop to rest the horses, their tails go up and they put some manure on the ground. But what happens when you stop a tractor? It just leaks oil out of the crankcase, and that doesn't do the ground any good!" Mention of tractors reminds me of a farmers' witticism: "There is nothing so pitiful as seeing a horsefly sitting on a tractor trying to bite it."

My parents' first two cars were Maxwells, which were very unpredictable. I still have my parents' mohair auto robe, in good condition, made by "Strook" around 1920. Whenever we drove a Maxwell up our steep grade, everyone but the driver had to get out and push. Our third car was our first reliable one, a 1925 Chevrolet sedan.

I remember many household changes in my parents' day too. A bathroom was installed in the house to replace the outhouse--a real improvement in cold, rainy weather. The telephone company switched us from the old 20- party line, with hand-cranked phones, to a dial system ten-party line which was split in half so that only five families heard each other's rings. Thus the number of possible curious listeners to your conversation was reduced from nineteen to four. Electric lights replaced kerosene and gasoline lamps and lanterns in our house and barn. An electric refrigerator replaced the cool pit in the ground under the back porch. In the 1930s we acquired an electric range, but kept the old wood range for heat in the winter.

Religion was an important factor in my parents' lives. After his conversion experience my father was rather zealous about religion for several decades. Mother told me, with some disdain, about the time he tried to convert a neighbor, John Childers. Father said, "John, you ought to become a Christian. It will make a better man of you." Mr. Childers replied with some anger, "I'm a good man now!" And he was.

In 1917 my parents joined Leslie Methodist Episcopal Church on south Commercial Street in Salem. Why did they join Leslie instead of First Methodist Church, also in Salem and a mile nearer to our farm? Perhaps they preferred the minister or the smaller, less affluent congregation. They became close friends with the minister, Reverend Aldrich, and his wife and daughter. A standing arrangement developed whereby Leslie's Ladies Aid Society drove out to our farm each spring for an all-day picnic. Thanks to our intensive preparations for the affair, more cleaning, repairs, and painting were done in and around the house then than in all the rest of the year.

Father had a habit of going to sleep during the sermons. Considering his daily rising at 5 A.M. and his sitting in a warm church after working in the cold outdoor air, sleepiness was only natural. Nevertheless, Mother and I felt embarrassed, so we sat, one on each side of him, taking turns at poking him in the ribs with our elbows to wake him up. Looking back at it it now, I wish we had let the poor man sleep. Some of the sermons were not very good anyway! The membership of Leslie Church dwindled in recent decades, and in 1981 the congregation disbanded. Four years later the building was torn down.

Father had a major accident around 1920. Nearly every year we baled and stored in our barn red clover hay to sell the following winter. Mother or I led a horse back and forth to hoist the bales, one at a time, up to the haymow where Father, hayhooks in hand, pulled them in and stacked them. This time he reached out too far, lost his balance, and fell 25 feet to the wood floor of the driveway. He landed in a sitting position, permanently pushing one hip higher than the other, a condition which caused him some pain the rest of his life.

Mother was in poor health through most of the 1920s. She had high blood pressure and varicose veins, and I am sure that the hard work and unhappy marriage were major causes. Family arguments increased in frequency around 1930. Mother was convinced (erroneously, I believe) that Father did not love her, and his sister Vestilla had continued to be a negative influence. Father did not help the situation with his oft-stated excuse: "That's the way I am; I can't change!" I generally took Mother's side.

At the end of my freshman year in college (summer, 1932) Mother got a divorce; tension had reached the point that it seemed to be the only solution. But the divorce was rough on everyone. Difficult financially, for it happened in the midst of the Great Depression. Difficult emotionally, for in spite of the misunderstandings, my parents still loved each other as long as they lived. Neither ever remarried.

The divorce settlement was that Mother was to pay Father for half of all personal property, including the livestock and machinery. She kept the farm because she had bought it with her own money. Considering all the work Father had put into improving the farm, including his help in constructing the buildings, I realize now that the settlement was not fair to him. For the next two years he worked for a dairy farmer at Tillamook, Oregon. Next, he bought and operated a ten-acre chicken ranch near Marysville, Washington, for he still had relatives in the region. During World War II he added to his work load by taking a job in an ammunition depot located, I believe, between Marysville and Everett.

In 1943 he had a hernia operation in the General Hospital in Everett. A few days later I drove up to see him, in spite of the gasoline rationing; I carried cans of gasoline in the trunk of the car. Hospitals had not yet adopted the practice of exercising patients as soon as possible after an operation. The nurses first asked him to get up for exercise on August 9, a week after the operation. As he started to do so, he said, "I don't feel very well," then fell back in bed, dead from a blood clot on the brain at the age of 66.

After the divorce, Mother and I operated our dairy for a year, both of us milking the thirteen cows by hand. The following school year (1933-34) we leased out the farm, equipped with the livestock and machinery, and rented a house in Salem while I returned to Willamette University for my sophomore year. Leasing the farm turned out to be a disaster. We made the same type of naive mistake that Grandfather Branchflower had made: we trusted the renters because they were members of our church. But the father and son were lazy, did not keep the farm in repair, and to save money, starved our horses. The horses became so hungry that they actually gnawed wood off their mangers.

As soon as the lease expired, Mother and I moved back to the farm. I had neither the time nor the money then to attend college, and we concentrated on repairing buildings, fences, and machinery. We sold the herd of cows (except one to provide our milk) and finished paying off the debt to Father. Disposal of the herd paved the way for me to attend Willamette while operating the farm for the next three years. At the same time we shifted our crops from grain and hay to grain and field and vegetable seeds.

Mother and I continued to live on the farm through World War II. In the fall of 1947 we sold the farm and settled her in a house in Salem containing rental apartments so that she would be financially independent. She was not very happy there, for the house needed much repair, renting apartments was a source of worry, and I was away for nine months (more on that later). On March 10, 1949, Mother died of a stroke at the age of 71. Both parents are buried in Belcrest Memorial Park near Salem.

In spite of the disharmony and divorce, both parents were really fine persons. Both were ethical, concerned for the welfare of others, friendly, industrious, and cultured. Neither one ever swore or told off-color stories. Both loved to read, but neither had much time to do it.

Nevertheless, each had individual weaknesses. Mother was inclined to be an introvert, too sensitive, too easily offended. Father was too temperamental, too insensitive, lacking in sound, practical judgment.

Each had individual strengths too. Mother had good judgment; she faced problems calmly and solved them. Although she was timid, she mustered the necessary courage in an emergency. Strong empathy for the unfortunate anywhere in the world was one of her traits. If she read in the morning paper of a great disaster somewhere, she would be sad all day. In contrast to Mother, Father was an extrovert; he loved to talk to strangers and old friends alike. He was courageous by nature. With him, intellectual curiosity was a passion. A minor manifestation of it was his practice whenever we vacationed in a resort town; he would arise before 6 A.M. and walk through the streets, examining the shop windows. Later in the day he would question the inhabitants to learn all about the town.

How could two such fine people end their marriage with a divorce? Misunderstanding, I believe, was the main factor, which began as the result of Aunt Tillie's counsel to Father and grew with the tension between his insensitive nature and Mother's sensitive nature. Although both parents were religious, religion did not solve their matrimonial problem.

4

CHILDHOOD AND YOUTH

I was born in our farmhouse December 29, 1911.

My earliest memory is that of an incident which occurred when I was three years old. My parents took me along when they attended the Panama-Pacific Exposition in 1915. I remember that a seal in a small tank had the nerve to splash water on me--a mean trick! Years later my parents told me that at the fair I scared the wits out of them by wandering off in the crowd and getting lost.

When I was four years old, we traveled by train to visit Aunt Sarah and Uncle Sandy Munro and their large family near Chilliwack, British Columbia. I remember that funloving Uncle Sandy played a prank on me. He invited me to play a game with him and instructed me to say "Just like me" after each sentence as he told a simple story. I naively obeyed, and when he uttered the punch line, "And there I saw a monkey," I responded, "Just like me." Everyone roared with laughter--except me! My cousin Douglas Munro has told me that also on that visit his father asked me my name, and as I pronounced it, Howard Merle Teeple came out "Hard Marl

Teebole." Uncle Sandy never tired of asking for repeat performances of that one.

Father returned to our farm, while Mother and I stayed longer with the Munros. According to a postcard he sent to her, he arrived in Salem September 21, 1916, stayed there overnight, and returned to the farm the next forenoon. I presume that my parents had started their trip by driving the eight miles to Salem in their horse and buggy, which were kept until Father's return at the livery stable at Front and Center Streets, at the foot of the bridge. The Portland Electric railroad station and a hotel were nearby on Front Street, enabling travelers to make connections easily; the boat landing on the Willamette River was also close by. When Mother and I began our journey homeward, riding on the train from Chilliwack to Vancouver, British Columbia, we passed numerous ponds, streams, and tiny waterfalls. I remember that I kept chanting, "Water, water, all the way."

When I was six, Father showed me pictures in a book and explained them to me, a few each evening. The book consisted of photographs of World War I. Not the best choice of subject matter, but a timely topic, for it was the last year of the war.

While I was seven my chief playmate, Ted, a beautiful white collie dog, died of old age. Father hitched our horse Dolly to a sled, loaded Ted's body on it, and drove half a mile down into the river-bottom portion of our farm. There, in sandy soil under three Douglas fir trees we buried Ted, with my tears. Father said simply, "You were a good dog, Ted; we'll miss you." Best funeral I ever attended--no theological nonsense, just love.

My parents replaced Ted with a handsome shepherd puppy which they named "Sport." Sport was very intelligent. Father let our cans of milk cool as long as possible in the morning. When he saw the milk truck coming to haul away the cans, he put the cans in a cart and ran out to the road, pushing the cart ahead of him. By the time Sport was grown, that dog understood the excitement. Distinguishing the sound of the milk truck from that of all other motor vehicles, he would bark to alert Father long before we could see the truck come around the bend in the road. Sport also got his picture in a national magazine. The *Farm Journal* had an essay contest for farm boys and girls on the subject of their hobby, and I wrote about my stamp collecting. I sent along a photograph Father had taken of Sport and me on a teeterboard. Thanks to Sport's good looks, our picture was published in the magazine, but my essay did not win any prize.

My cousin Kenneth, who was five years older than I, laughed at me for still believing in Santa Claus when I was seven. My parents taught me to tell the truth always, and I was shocked to learn that they had lied to me. If I had children, I would not tell them that there is really a Santa Claus.

When I was seven or eight, our neighbors, the Julian Strattons, acquired the first radio in the community. At their invitation I went to their home one afternoon to listen to a children's program broadcast from that powerful radio station in Pittsburgh, KDKA. Later we acquired a five-tube Atwater Kent radio, with a separate crook-neck speaker. When I stop to think that in my lifetime I have seen technology go from the beginnings of radio to the prevalence of home computers and camcorders, I realize that I must be getting old.

When I was young, children had fewer toys than today, but those few were loved dearly. I had only two animal toys: "Teddy," my teddy bear, and "Quackie," my wooden duck. Quackie was brightly painted, with jointed legs and neck; with the greatest of ease, he could walk forward while looking backward, or vice versa. My favorite books were several in the "Billy Whiskers" series. In my day children made many of their own toys, an activity that was as much fun as playing with them. Playmates taught me how to make wooden swords for duels. With their help I made small wooden cars and trucks, with wheels made by sawing off short sections of a broom handle. And, of course, these vehicles had to have lots of roads to run on, complete with road signs and bridges, up hills and around curves. My favorite home-made toys were my bow and arrows, made from hazelnut and arrowwood bushes and a yew tree, all of which grew on our farm.

The diversity of the topography on the farm provided a playground with more variety than most farms. The upland woods, the steep wooded bank, and the river bottom differed greatly from each other and invited exploration. The slough at the foot of the bank furnished boating and fishing.

In 1975 I walked around on the farm again. I was dismayed at the changes made since Mother sold it in 1947. All of the buildings, except the house, had been torn down. The farm had been resold several times, and the second new owner had cut down the trees and sold the logs for lumber. Gone was the grove behind the barn where I had often played and the livestock had found shelter from the winter rain and the summer sun. Gone was the grove at the end of the lane, and gone was the long row of majestic Douglas fir trees along the top of the bank, trees which added much to the beauty of the farm. The third new owner had cleared the rest of the river-bottom land, and the delightful picnic area along the slough was gone forever. This owner, who had converted the farm to the raising of beef cattle, kept cattle in a fattening shed which he rarely cleaned, forcing the cattle in it to stand continually or lie down in sloppy filth a foot deep. This would never have happened under my father's management, for he cleaned and swept the barn daily and put straw bedding in the animals' stalls each night. Eagerness for profits had replaced concern for aesthetics and the comfort of live stock. I came away from the farm feeling very sad. I never want to visit the place again. It just doesn't seem like home anymore.

In order to give me the best education they could, my parents arranged for me to attend public schools in Salem instead of the one-room country school in our community, Spring Valley. Another reason for the arrangement was the fact that the country school was a mile and a half from our farm. I was seven when I began school in 1919. Mother rented an apartment in the

McAlpine Apartments on Center Street in Salem while I attended the old Washington School for the first grade. Father drove in the eight miles on Friday nights to take us back to the farm for the weekends. Mother then cooked and baked for Father to carry him through the next week, and on Sunday evenings he took us back to the apartment. Mother and I moved back to the farm for the summer. At that time my parents thought the effort worthwhile and bought a house in Salem on south Liberty Street (a fire station now stands on the lot), and I attended Lincoln School for my second and third grades. By the end of my third school year, however, Mother and Father had had enough of the separation from each other and the frequent driving back and forth. So they sold the house, and Mother and I moved back to the farm permanently. Thereafter I went to Spring Valley School until I graduated from the eighth grade in 1927.

Some pre-teenage boys go through a stage when they dislike girls; that was never my problem, for I liked both boys and girls. In the first grade I thought Pauline Pruner was very nice when some of us played by the hedge in front of her house. I still remember how happy I was when Marjorie Webb, an undertaker's daughter, smiled at me when we were in the third grade at Lincoln School. While in the second and third grades, two boys were my constant playmates, Leonard and Ralph. Also, while I was attending school in Salem, a little girl next door who could not say "Howard" called me "How" and later changed to "Ard"; we moved back to the farm before she ever got it all together.

Country school was quite different from city school, and I am glad that I experienced both. In the country one teacher in a one-room schoolhouse taught all eight grades daily; thus each grade received her attention only a fraction of the time. In the city, however, the pupils in each grade received a teacher's attention all day, and therefore more information could be taught. In the country one class after another sat on the recitation bench immediately in front of the teacher's desk. While one class was reciting, the rest of us were supposed to be studying our textbooks, but sometimes we listened to what was going on up front. Thus in the country we remembered better what we were taught, for we were exposed to it many times. Also, in the country we played with pupils of all ages, not just those in our own grade.

Our rural community in general had resented my parents' sending me to a city school. One neighbor lady had remarked, "The Teeples think their kid is too good to go to country school!" A few weeks after I entered the country school, the community resentment was manifested by a schoolmate, Vernon Windsor. As Vernon and I were walking home from school, he went to the side of the road, pulled out his jackknife, and began to cut a briar about eight or ten feet long. I saw what was coming, so I took out my jackknife and cut a similar briar for myself. Then we took off our coats and began to whip each other with the briars. After we had worn out four or five briars apiece, we called it quits. Both of us were "battered but unbowed." We were bleeding and our clothes were torn. Vernon remarked, "I thought you'd be a sissy because you went to school in town, but you're as tough as the rest of us!" After that, Vernon and I became good friends.

Today, every time I think of Vernon, I begin to chuckle. He got me into more trouble than all my other playmates combined. The first time occurred when I accompanied Father on a visit to Vernon's father to buy wheat for planting. At Vernon's suggestion we played in a strawstack in which his father's hogs had nests. Soon dozens of fleas were biting me! When we got home, Father took me behind the woodshed (no, he did not paddle me) and we got rid of the fleas by both of us stripping off our clothes and taking a shower under the overflow pipe from our water tank in the woodshed.

Once Vernon and I were walking through the woods on my farm and, spying a yellow jackets' nest in a tree, he thought it would be fun to throw sticks at it. We did, and the whole colony attacked us. I have never been stung so much in my life--by bees, that is.

One year at Spring Valley School a class was on the recitation bench for an English lesson. When asked to supply the correct form of the verb "break" in the sentence "The chair was _____ ," Edwin Schubert said "broke." The teacher said, "No, that's not right. Vernon, what should he have said?" Vernon said the same thing his father would have said, "busted." Many of us were listening in, and we "busted" out in laughter.

Vernon and Halloween were made for each other. In those good old days there was none of this sissy trick or treat stuff. We didn't give our victims any choice. On Halloween Vernon and I went around the community as a team, and the neighbors kept their fingers crossed, wondering, "What the heck will those kids think of this year?" The least obnoxious of our late-night tricks included writing "Guess who was here?" on windows with soap, running around houses yelling like Indians, and moving gates and livestock around. These pranks were not as easy as they appear, for every farmer had at least one watchdog, and there was many a contest between boys' brains and dogs' brains. Vernon had a couple of brainstorms that afterwards I was sorry I had participated in. One was for me to drive my parents' car down the road with Vernon sitting beside me, and whenever we came to a mailbox, he stuck out one of his big feet and let it knock the box off its post. The other mistake was intended as innocent fun, but did not turn out that way in one case. Vernon thought it would be great to drive around at midnight, pick up stones from the road, and throw them on the upper portion of roofs so that they would roll down with a clatter guaranteed to awaken any snoring farmer. The scheme worked fine, until at one house I accidently threw a stone through the glass window of the front door. Ashamed of myself, I voluntarily went there the next morning and paid for replacement of the glass. I do not know what were the sins of my father's youth that caused his conversion, but Halloween capers were the sins of my youth! They did not cause me to "get religion," however--I did not repent enough.

One year it was I instead of Vernon who came up with a brilliant idea for a Halloween prank. I had saved two Roman candles from the Fourth of July. So Vernon and I went to the Smith's house after dark to surprise the three children there, but sure that we would appear, they surprised us by hiding behind a woodpile. Then Vernon and I withdrew and each lit a Roman candle and swung it at arm's length in a vertical circle as we ran around the house yelling. Young Edgar ran into the house, crying out, "Mama, Mama, the boys are shooting guns!" If you want to have some fun, try mixing some Fourth of July into Halloween--or vice versa.

The Fourth of July was more fun in the old days too, with lots of firecrackers and a great variety of fireworks. A friendly contest developed through the years between the Smith children, who lived across the road, and me to see who could shoot off firecrackers the earlier on the morning of the Fourth. One year my father decided to settle the matter once for-all. He arose at four A.M., shot off his double-barreled shotgun, and crawled back into bed. I really think he violated the rules of the game.

Another buddy at Spring Valley School was Claude Walling. Claude was the first in the school to own that new invention, the Eversharp pencil. One day, when we were sitting at our desks, I tried to grab his new pencil, just to tease him. But he saw me coming and grabbed it first; all I got was the pencil top. After holding it awhile, I balanced the top on my thumbnail and snapped it toward the flies on the high ceiling. Seizing my geography book, I studied like mad while I listened for the top to hit the floor. But it never did. Then I looked around just in time to see Iris Smith clawing at something that had gone down her back! At recess she refused to give Claude his pencil top until I convinced her that it was all my fault, not his.

The Spring Valley Community Club was a delightful and beneficial factor in my life. Once a month during the school year all the neighbors in the Spring Valley School District met in the school house for entertainment, refreshments, and socializing. At Christmas time the schoolchildren put on the program and were rewarded with presents distributed by a well-padded Santa Claus. In May the meeting was a "Last-day-of-school picnic," which always ended with a baseball game. At the other meetings local talent provided a variety of entertainment, including vocal and instrumental music, recitations, and plays ranging from one act to three acts. A newspaper clipping I have reports that on March 11, 1927, when Father was president of the club, Marie Flint McCall, a pianist from the Brush College School District, played "Moonlight Revels," followed by an amusing story she told on the piano as an encore. Next came a three-act "rural comedy" entitled "Back to the Country Store," with a cast of nine of my neighbors. Between the acts Irene Windsor gave a comic monologue, "A Married Man Sewing on a Button;" four- year-old Elma Ray sang a solo; the Spring Valley Harmony Four (consisting of three of my schoolmates and myself) gave a burlesque rendition of "Marching Through Georgia." The club was as democratic as a club can be, for everyone who lived in the school district was automatically a member. When I became a college student, my appreciation of the arts became more sophisticated, and I tended to view with disdain the performances in the Community Club. After graduation, however, my appreciation of the club returned, for I began to realize that its purpose was not the production of art, but the promotion of fellowship and neighborhood unity--a goal the club achieved admirably.

Spring Valley School District was consolidated with Salem schools in 1954. The schoolhouse, built in 1907, is preserved today as the Spring Valley Community Center. I hold cherished memories of Spring Valley School, the Community Club, and our farm.

In 1925, when I was thirteen, my parents took Grandfather Branchflower, my fox terrier Zip (Sport had died), and me along on a visit to Mother's sister Sarah and family. Father drove our new Chevrolet sedan. En route home we stayed for a few days with Father's sister Tillie Bedford and family, while Grandfather remained with Aunt Sarah for a while. The Bedfords took us in their launch to their vacation and fishing shack on Whidbey Island. One night Uncle Jimmie Bedford and his son Charles took Father and me with them when they went fishing in Puget Sound. When they hauled in their net, they had the biggest haul of fish they had gotten all season. A thrilling experience for me!

The Bedfords raised New Zealand Red rabbits and gave me a pair which we took home in our car. Father constructed an ingenious chicken-wire cage, about six by eight feet in size, with no bottom, and a door on top. With the rabbits and their hutch inside, we moved the cage every two weeks to clean ground and fresh grass in our enormous backyard. The rabbits often tried to dig a hole at a corner of the cage. We put rocks in the hole because we thought they were trying to escape. Once we neglected to block the hole, and then we found out what the rabbits were really up to; they were burrowing to make a nest for mamma rabbit to give birth to her young; they preferred their underground nest to the one we had provided in their hutch. Soon we had too many rabbits, so we ate some. Tenderhearted Mother had qualms about eating these pets. She used to say, "When I am eating them, I can almost see their little eyes!"

Father gave me my first business experience while I was still quite young, for which I am grateful. He bought some weaner pigs, six weeks old, and turned them over to me to raise. I had to weigh and record the amount of his ground grain that I fed them. When I sold them, the net profit was mine, after I repaid him the cost of the pigs and grain. Incidentally, pigs are the most maligned of livestock. They are quite intelligent and, with the exception of cats and dogs, the only farm animals that can be trained to use one end of their pen as a toilet.

I have always enjoyed reading and learning. My parents had a bookcase full of books, most of which I read. They purchased for me the *World Book Encyclopedia,* which I used frequently. In those days farmers could borrow directly from the Oregon State Library in Salem, with access to the stacks. I had a binge of reading the fairy stories in that library. Father was worried and advised me to read better books, but I kept on until I finished the whole collection of them.

In the field of music I was untalented. When I was quite young, I took piano lessons from Mrs. McCall, a grand lady, but my heart was not in it. Later I took vocal lessons, but my throat was not with it, for I inherited from my father a sinus drip, which he called "catarrh." In college I enrolled in a music appreciation course, but dropped it after a week because I did not have the ear for it. Lacking the heart, throat, and ear, a great performer of music I was not destined to be!

Gradually I was exposed to conservative religion. On my eleventh birthday my parents gave me a copy of the King James, or Authorized, Version of the Bible; it was well worn by the time I finished high school. Although Grandfather taught me verses from "the good book," as he called the Bible, his interpretation of them was not fundamentalist. When I was twelve years old my parents became concerned that I had not been baptized. Therefore they had our minister, the Reverend Aldrich, perform the ceremony one Sunday. About that time they went through a pietistic period that lasted two years; in the winter evenings the three of us would take turns at reading from the Bible, followed by our kneeling beside our chairs and praying aloud.

Several factors led me into fundamentalism. My parents attended some of the revival meetings conducted by traveling evangelists at the Turner camp grounds. My untrained, but well-meaning, Sunday school teachers taught me that all of the Bible is true. I joined the David C. Cook organization for youth, the I.A.H. ("I Am His," i.e., Jesus') Club and wore the I.A.H. ring. After responding to an advertisement in the *Christian Herald* magazine, I took a correspondence course in Old Testament theology from the Moody Bible Institute in Chicago. The course was distinctly fundamentalist in point of view, accepting the premise that if one's soul is to be saved for heaven, it is fundamental, or necessary, to believe certain fundamentalist doctrines, including the inerrancy of the Bible. By the time I graduated from the eighth grade at Spring Valley, I was definitely a fundamentalist.

Yet, even then, I could not help observing that some very fine people were not fundamentalists. In fact, some were not even Christians, including two wonderful teachers, Mrs. Stalcup and Mrs. Sohn. Another non-Christian was our neighbor, Vivian Stratton, who donated more of his time to help others in need in Spring Valley than anyone else in the school district.

From the ninth to twelfth grades, inclusive, I rode the school bus to school in Salem. For the ninth grade I attended Parrish Junior High. All of us from country schools had to adjust to a large school with students who had had training and experiences we lacked. My main problem was playing basketball during gym periods. I had never had my hands on a basketball before--in fact, I had not even seen the game played. When I dribbled the ball, it seemed that the referee was always calling out, "Steps."

A close friend of mine, Howard Cross, organized about a dozen of us ninth-graders into a boys' club which he named "The Peps." Miss Reed, a teacher, was our advisor. I can't remember that we did much, except that one Sunday the members and their parents drove out to our farm and had a picnic at our picnic grounds. Howard assigned to each member an "Indian" name with the same initials as our real names. Since my initials were H.M.T., I was "Heap Mud Turtle." Howard Bert Cross became "Heap Big Crow."

During the next three years I attended Salem High School. At Parrish I had taken Latin, and in high school I took two more years of it. One year I was *Consul Primus,* president, of the Latin Club. My third year of Latin consisted of the translation of Cicero's orations, taught by a marvelous teacher, Joy Hills. In addition to guiding our translating, she led the class in discussing moral and philosophical questions commented on by Cicero. She demonstrated by her life and teaching that a non-religious person can have high ethical principles. In my senior year I was on the school's debate team. Otherwise I did nothing noteworthy except to get good grades. When I graduated in 1931, I was fifth in order for valedictorian and the only one among the 250 graduates who had received straight As in English through the ninth to twelfth grades.

The Peps had disbanded when we graduated from junior high, but we remained close friends in high school. Three of us of different heights would walk down the halls in formation. As the tallest, I was at one end, and Ralph Coulson, the shortest, at the other end; Howard Cross, of medium height, was in the middle. We called ourselves "The Three Steps."

Once in geometry class when the teacher was discussing a problem involving the legs of a triangle, she said, "I would use one of my legs for that." Billy Price, a Pep sitting beside me, started to laugh and the teacher asked, "What's so funny?" Billy replied, still laughing, "You said-- ha, ha--you said you'd use one of your legs!" The teacher remarked indignantly, "Well, I didn't know that anyone in the class would be evil-minded!" From then on we kidded Billy about his being "evil-minded."

While I was in elementary school, I had begun to paste in a notebook a sample of each year's Christmas seals, or "TB stamps," as I used to call them. The collection begins with the 1918 and 1919 stamps, which bear the name and symbol of the American Red Cross. Thereafter the stamps have the symbol of the National Tuberculosis Association. In the same notebook I wrote and pasted in poems and maxims, some serious, some humorous. This practice I continued sporadically in high school years. Afterwards I was surprised to find that my father had pasted similar material in his college notebook. I still have a large collection of buttons of the boys and girls clubs I joined, clubs promoted by radio and magazines.

"Tall tales" appealed to me, and I collected and told them for fun. Father, and occasionally Mother, told jokes, but never tall tales. I was fascinated by humor of all kinds: the radio programs of Fred Allen, Eddie Cantor, George

Burns and Gracie Allen, and Fibber Magee and Molly; the Charlie Chaplin and Laurel and Hardy movies; the wit of Will Rogers, "Bill Nye," and the "Sayings of Mr. Dooley;" the stories by P. G. Wodehouse. I memorized comic rhymes such as (authors unknown to me):

Troubles
Adam
Had 'em.

Wisdom
When I was young and had no sense,
I very easily took offence;
But now I'm old and grown more wise--
I only fight with the little guys.

I was an active member of the Epworth League at Leslie Church, and in the summers of 1930 and 1931 I attended the Epworth League Institute held annually in the wooded campground near Falls City, a logging town at the edge of the Coast Range Mountains. There for a week we Leaguers attended religious classes in the forenoon, played games in the afternoon, and attended religious services in the evening, followed by an informal meeting around the campfire in each church's own camp. At the final evening service each year an appeal was made for us to prayerfully listen for the Spirit of Jesus to call us to a life of Christian service as a minister or missionary. In 1931, just after graduation from high school, I responded to the appeal. I did not hear a voice, but I felt an urge, which I regarded as a divine "call" to become a minister. Therefore I "went forward"with a few others and stood before the altar.

5

WILLAMETTE AND THE FARM

Another event in the summer after high school graduation was my brief visit to Willamette University, a Methodist school in Salem, to look over the campus after I had been admitted to become a freshman in the fall. I stopped in at the office of the president, Dr. Carl Gregg Doney, to ask for suggestions on how to prepare for college. He said that if I would keep a daily diary of my thoughts, rather than events, that "Some day you will become a bishop, pope, or something." I presume that the reason that I never became "a bishop, pope, or something" is that I kept the diary for only three days. Subsequently I did add from time to time my ideas for possible books, poems, songs, and radio shows that I might write someday. Now I am astonished at how pietistic are some of the religious ideas and how foolish are some of the humorous ideas. Some of the ethical ideas are sound, however. The entries in the notebook that were made in my later college years are more sensible than the earlier ones.

Dr. Doney's suggestion did succeed in one respect: it implanted the idea that thinking is very important. He also told me bluntly that I was "a lazy speaker," that is, that I did not enunciate well enough. (Later I tried to correct that fault when I majored in speech and drama.)

After I had decided to become a minister, the first step was for me to receive a Local Preacher's License. Normally the license was granted by one's own Methodist church at a quarterly conference which was presided over by the district superintendent. I had a little problem: Willamette University gave a tuition discount to students with the license, but Leslie Church would not have a quarterly conference until after school started. Therefore Dr. Carl Marcy, our district superintendent, took me to the September quarterly conference of the Methodist church in Silverton, Oregon, which bestowed the license. The license gave me authority to preach sermons in Leslie, which I did a few Sunday evenings. I must confess that I did not know what I was talking about, although at the time I sincerely thought I did.

Leslie Church supported a small country Methodist church at Roberts, six miles south of Salem. Our minister, the Reverend Darlow Johnson, Sr., asked me to preach there one Sunday. I decided to include in my public prayer something that I had read in the *Christian Herald*: "Lord, help us to hate the sin and love the sinner." In my nervousness I mixed it up and prayed, "Lord, help us to love the sin and hate the sinner!" One gentleman in the congregation roared with laughter. I hastily corrected myself, and then, very embarrassed, stumbled through the rest of my prayer.

Unaware of the fundamentalist-modernist controversy in Christianity, I bumped into it without realizing what was going on. Reverend Johnson was a tactful liberal Methodist who often incorporated thoughts from Leslie Weatherhead in his sermons. Once when I visited him in his study, I was shocked when he said that the Psalms were not necessarily written by David. He said, correctly, that the author ascriptions in the Bible were added long after the Psalms were written.

As a holder of a Local Preacher's License, I was invited to attend the monthly meetings of the Salem Ministerial Association. At one of the meetings a fundamentalist preacher asked the Reverend Parker, the modernist minister of the First Methodist Episcopal Church, whether he was a fundamentalist or a modernist. Reverend Parker replied, "I am modern enough to believe in all that is fundamental!" Again, I did not understand what was involved.

When I enrolled at Willamette University, I attended the school's reception for freshmen. There I visited with Roy Lockenour, a professor in Willamette's School of Law. In our conversation he mentioned favorably the theory of evolution, and I remarked, "But it can't be true! The Bible says the world was created in six days." Instead of arguing with me, he tactfully changed the subject. In my ignorance and conceit, I imagined that I had refuted a law professor.

While a freshman, I wrote an essay protesting the university's requirement that certain courses be taken before graduation. By the time I graduated, however, I realized how wrong I had been. Today I think that everyone should have a basic knowledge of language, science, history, sociology, economics, political science, and history of religion. If there is not time in college to take all the essential courses, one should buy or borrow introductory textbooks on the subjects and read them after graduation.

A course required of freshmen at Willamette then was "Bible History," taught by Professor Daniel H. Schulze, an ordained Methodist minister with a Ph.D. in religion from the University of Chicago. It was my first taste of historical study of the Bible. It shook me up psychologically, but the experience was invaluable. I am greatly indebted to Professor Schulze, for his teaching opened my eyes to the fallacy of fundamentalism, thereby changing the direction of my life. His course made possible a further awakening in Professor Clark's course a few years later.

I felt--perhaps erroneously--that laymen would not stand for it if I preached what I was now fully convinced was the truth. On the other hand, I could not conscientiously preach what I knew was false. Therefore, at the close of my sophomore year, I abandoned the goal of becoming a minister. Some of the laymen at Leslie Church blamed the university; I blamed the laymen and the fundamentalist movement.

In my junior year at Willamette I took the two-semester course, "Records of the Life of Jesus," taught by Herman Clark. The textbook, with the same title, was a synopsis of the synoptic gospels compiled by Henry Burton Sharman. Looking back on it from the standpoint of my present knowledge, I realize that the course had two weaknesses. First, the point of view of both Sharman and Clark was that of "nineteenth-century Christian liberalism," which held that Jesus, though human, was perfect. That view idealized Jesus and failed to recognize his Jewish nationalism and belief in Jewish eschatology, that is, the belief in the coming end of the world and a judgment day. Second, neither Sharman nor Clark knew the environment of the gospels, except a little of the Jewish milieu; knowledge of the environment is absolutely essential for understanding the gospels.

Nevertheless, the course had two remarkable strengths. First, it was taught in a completely open-minded manner, and students were encouraged to think for themselves. Second, the teaching method demonstrated the necessity of factual information. Professor Clark would ask a question about the text; we students would speculate as best we could; then he would give us a few pertinent facts and we could see how mistaken we had been when we lacked essential information. All the students were enthusiastic about the course, especially its method and the freedom allowed in the discussions. By the end of the course the students, including myself, generally accepted the liberal point of view, although we differed among ourselves in our selection from the gospel traditions of what is authentic, that is, of what is an accurate report of what Jesus said and did.

The course revived my interest in religion and left me wanting to know more. What did Jesus actually say? What did he actually do? Just how did Christianity really begin?

I had stopped going to Leslie Church, but some of my college classmates persuaded me to join "The Vespers," a student group at the First Methodist Church. This group met at the church on Sunday evenings and held two weekend camping trips annually: in the Cascade Mountains on the Fourth of July, and at the Oregon coast on Labor Day. The camping sites varied from year to year. People who live in the Willamette Valley have the advantage of being within easy driving distance of mountain resorts to the east and seaside resorts to the west.

The members of The Vespers were wonderful young people, and some fine friendships were formed. I dated several of the girls and soon settled on one, Mary Farnum. She was the one who planned the food to take on camping trips, and she always did it well. She and I were really in love with each other, but there was an important problem. A successful marriage must appeal to both the heart and the head, but this romance did not appeal to our heads. I was the studious type, but Mary did not want to concentrate that much. We had difficulty in discussing serious topics. Yet I could not force myself to end the courtship; eventually Mary wisely took that step.

In 1937 I represented Willamette University in the Pacific Coast Intercollegiate After-Dinner-Speaking contest. A criterion in the judging was adaptation to the occasion. The contest was held in the basement banquet room of the Quelle Cafe in Salem, and someone had had the strange notion of decorating the ceiling by shingling it. The student from the University of Southern California won the contest with his opening remark: "I have heard that it rains a lot in western Oregon, but I did not realize until tonight that it rains so hard that they have to shingle the ceiling of basements!"

Saving enough money to attend college was difficult in those days. One had to pay one's own way because scholarships, grants, and loans were scarce. After my sophomore year I had to stay home another year and could enroll only part-time when I did attend. Finally, in 1938, seven years after I had begun, I graduated, not *cum laude,* but come what may. I did not study very hard, for I had to operate the farm while I was in college. Also, I saw no need to strain myself getting A grades, for I had no intention of going on to graduate school.

The divorce in the family forced me to manage the farm myself. I thought management would be easy for, after all, I had grown up on that farm, worked on it, and observed my father's management. Nevertheless, my first year was a partial failure because I was late with the planting and harvesting. I got behind with the work in the spring and was unable to catch up all season. If crops are not planted on time, the ground is too dry and little growth results. If the crops are not harvested on time, they become too ripe--hay becomes tough and grain and seed crops shatter on the ground before harvesting. My basic fault was that I began each day by asking myself, "What should I do today?" I should have asked, "What is the most *urgent work* that I should do today?" After 1936, however, I prospered at farming.

During the Great Depression farm wages in Oregon were generally twenty-five cents an hour, although one year the rate was only twenty cents. The fact that the Willamette Valley produced so much fruit and vegetables in addition to meat and dairy products alleviated the conditions there.

Unemployment was not a problem for farmers, for on a farm there was always work to be done. A young neighbor expressed it this way during the Depression: "Sometimes I wish I lived in town, where I would have to go around looking for work, instead of living on a farm, where the work is always looking for me!"

Searching for crops that would be more profitable than hay and grain, I shifted some of our fields to the production of vegetable seeds and of two field seeds, Chewings fescue and crimson clover. Chewings fescue is a lawn grass widely used for golf courses. Production of vegetable seeds required much hand labor, and I employed several dozen men and women from the Dust Bowl of the Midwest who had migrated to the West Coast to find work. I worked beside them in the field, hoeing, crawling on hands and knees to plant onion bulbs six inches apart in trenches, and picking onion seed by snapping off the heads by hand. As an employer, I understood the employer's point of view, and by working beside and talking with the workers, I learned their point of view also. Everyone while young should have some experience on each side of the fence: as a laborer and as an employer.

For many years I was uncertain what my future vocation would be. Although I was a successful farmer, I did not want to remain a farmer. I wanted a vocation that was independent of the weather and above all, more stimulating intellectually. Thinking that perhaps I should be a high school teacher, I attended the University of Oregon for a winter term, taking education courses. A professor there convinced me that, because I had not studied education at Willamette, with about the same amount of study I could get a Master's degree in the field of my undergraduate major, speech, and teach in college. Accepting his advice, I returned to the farm, intending to save up money for earning a Master in speech therapy at the University of Washington. But something happened that ended the plan: the attack on Pearl Harbor.

The draft board deferred me because I was the only man in the family to operate the farm. An additional reason was that I grew vegetable seeds, essential for the following year's food production. During the war the United States shipped tons of vegetable seeds to its allies, including the Soviet Union. Farming then was difficult because of the shortage of labor, which made it necessary for farmers to exchange work at harvest time. When I worked for my neighbors to repay them for helping me, my own fields were neglected. That was not the situation before the war when I could hire workers from town or from small ten-acre tracts in my community.

The most important development in my life in this period between college graduation and marriage was the investigation of Christian origins. How does one proceed in such a search? Soon after graduation, I began by reading books and by examining the New Testament more closely. I borrowed books from the Oregon State Library, Willamette University's library, Salem Public Library, and Portland Public Library. The goal at first was merely to satisfy my curiosity.

The first library book I read was George
Lamsa's *Gospel Light,* a bad choice. The author
assumed that Near Eastern customs in the twentieth century are still the same as they were in the
first century, and that therefore the customs today
help us to understand the teaching of Jesus. This
is a risky assumption because some of the customs
have changed. A more reliable procedure is to
use ancient evidence, such as contemporary
Palestinian archaeology and contemporary Near
Eastern writings.   Lamsa also made the mistake
of trying to prove that the canonical gospels were
originally written in Aramaic, a theory that is
definitely false. When I read the book, however,
I thought it was a good one, but I lacked the
knowledge of the field that is essential for proper
evaluation.   That experience demonstrated the
danger of becoming too enthusiastic about a book
(or magazine article or newspaper report) when
one does not know enough about the subject.

The next book I read, however, was very
helpful. It was *The Search for the Real Jesus* , by
Chester C. McCown, professor of New Testament
and director of the Palestine Institute at the
Pacific School of Religion in Berkeley. The author summarized the efforts during the preceding
one hundred years to find out what Jesus actually
said and did--the same quest that I was beginning.
By using the bibliographies and notes in the books
I read, along with the card catalog in libraries, I
compiled a list of 200 relevant books, most of
which I read. I still have the well-worn sheets of
that list.

In winter I read library books all day and in
summer (except during the war years) in the

evening. I read slowly, thinking about the material, investigating biblical references, and taking many notes. Some notes were written at the relevant place in Sharman's synopsis, my textbook in Professor Clark's course. Sometimes I spent as much as an hour in reading one page, for I investigated as I read. While routinely driving the tractor, I often pondered what I had read the night before. Taking time to think about what one reads is very important.

When I was reading Jewish history as background of the gospels, I made the mistake of stopping when the history reached A.D. 30, the approximate date of Jesus' death. Later I learned that the gospels were not written until the last quarter of the first century A.D. Therefore knowledge of Jewish, Roman, and Christian history in the whole first century is relevant for gospel study. Awareness of the influence of the Christian environment upon the writing of the New Testament gradually broadened my search from asking "What did Jesus say and do?" to include "What was going on in the churches in the New Testament period?"

Another discovery that surprised me was the enormous scope of the knowledge essential for understanding the Bible. When I began to investigate I thought that I would have to read only a few books to accomplish my goal, but the more I read, the more I realized that there was still so much to learn. A further valuable lesson was the realization that the diversity of interpretations of the Bible demonstrates the necessity of objective study if one is to penetrate the maze of opinions and find the truth. A book that gave me an excellent overview of the history of religion and culture in general was *An Intellectual and Cultural History of the Western World,* by Harry Elmer Barnes.

In the winter of 1946-1947 I drove to Salem one evening each week to attend an Oregon State University extension course on Oregon history. The professor had put some books on reserve at the Salem Public Library, and I drove in early so that I could study them before class. Gladys Windedahl was on duty at the circulation desk, and I soon decided that with her beauty, brains, and personality, she ought to be the woman for me. I thought that the proper procedure would be to get acquainted before asking for a date, but how can one visit with a busy librarian in a library? I had an idea. When I had taken notes from reading books about the Bible, I had made the mistake of writing on both sides of the paper. The notes on one side needed to be retyped so that all could be cut apart and rearranged. As a way of getting acquainted, I asked Miss Windedahl if I could hire her to do the retyping. She replied that she was not an expert typist, but she had a friend who was and would like some spare-time work at home. I was stuck! I had to go ahead and hire her married friend, Mrs. Dorothy Nolan, to do the typing.

Undaunted, I mustered my courage in March and asked Gladys if I could take her to dinner. On our second date we went to a movie, and when I took her home, she invited me into the house for a toasted cheese sandwich and hot chocolate, which were delicious. Jokingly, Gladys has said since that was how she landed me! Within a few days I was head—over—heels in love with her. Here was a woman who appealed to both my heart and head.

Religion was a potential problem in our courtship. She was an active member of St. Mark's Lutheran Church in Salem and sang in the choir. I was unorthodox and not a member of any church at the time. I explained my views to Gladys and told her of my intense desire to learn the truth about the beginning of Christianity. She listened with interest, and showed me a book she had had as a textbook at Augustana College in Sioux Falls, namely, *Christianity and Liberalism,* by J. G. Machen. The author, a religious conservative, wrote it to denounce Christian liberalism. Her other courses at Augustana were not that narrow-minded, thank goodness. The book made me wonder if Gladys was really the woman for me, after all, but I could see that she was a reasonable person, willing to learn. On the other hand, she wondered about me, but when she conferred with her pastor, the Reverend Mark Getzendaner, he assured her that "Christianity needs thinkers." Gladys' mother too was sensible and fair-minded and readily accepted me. My mother and Gladys readily accepted each other too; both held similar religious beliefs, so religion was no problem between them.

Three months after Gladys and I began going together, we became engaged. I wanted to get married very soon, for our romance had such a late start--she was 39 and I was 35. But Gladys wisely recognized that we must first put our affairs in order. Her mother worked at Willamette

University, and she and Gladys owned their house which contained two rental apartments. Thus her mother would be self-supporting without Gladys. My mother and I had decided the previous year that we wanted to sell the farm and live in town, and this summer we sold it. The large house in Salem that she bought had two rental apartments in it besides the main floor, which Mother occupied. She and I worked hard at cleaning and repairing the house, which was in terrible condition. I converted two bedrooms and large closets into two more rental apartments to provide Mother with more income.

At last, on October 26, 1947, Gladys and I were married by Reverend Getzendaner in St. Mark's. An old friend of her family told me afterwards that I had "got a good one," and time proved he was right. Our honeymoon was a week at the Oregon coast in La Vista Terrace Motel at Ocean Lake, with seagulls in the air and waves splashing on huge rocks just outside our picture window.

What kind of ancestors did Gladys have? How religious were they?

Gladys Windedahl Teeple

6

GLADYS' ANCESTORS

Gladys' ancestors, both maternal and paternal, came from Norway. They came to America as separate families from various locations southeast of the eastern end of the Sognefjord.

Norway is noted for its many small coves located along the banks of its numerous fjords. The word "Viking" is derived from the Norwegian term for a cove, *vik*. To "go viking" in the summer originally meant to go on an expedition, from cove to cove, to explore and plunder. The Vikings grew in power and dominated the seas for two and a half centuries (ca. 800-1066). Many migrated to nearby lands; some sailed into the Mediterranean and brought home slaves and wives, especially from Italy. Some dark-haired Norwegians and Norwegian Americans today are descendants of that mixture of Norse and Mediterranean blood; my wife Gladys is probably one of them.

Tillable land is scarce in mountainous Norway, and what little exists has been divided into "farms" much too small to support a family. It is important to distinguish between two types of "farmers" in Norway in the past. The *bonde,* or owner, lived in a relatively large house on the farm, and the farm usually had a name. In many cases a few small houses, each with a tiny garden plot, were on the farm. These small houses, or tenant farms, were leased by the owner on a semi-permanent basis, to *husmenn,* that is, tenant farmers, or cotters. These tenant farms had names too. Today, thanks to a law which permits it, the inhabitants of these small plots may own them instead of leasing them. The little tenant farms could hardly support a family, and a *husmann* found work away from home whenever he could.

Personal names were formed in this manner: If Lars had a son and named him Olaf, the boy's name was Olaf Larsson (or Larson or Larsen), and if Olaf had a son Johannes, that son's name was Johannes Olafson. In the case of a daughter, "datter" or "dotter" instead of "son" or "sen" was attached as a suffix to the father's name, for example, Olafsdatter. Many dialects existed in Norway, resulting in much variation in both spelling and pronunciation. Also, the Danish occupation (15th-18th c.) led to the adoption of the Oslo dialect of Danish as the official language, known as *riksmaal,* or *bokmaal,* or Dano-Norwegian. In the middle of the nineteenth century Ivar Aasen, motivated by patriotism, produced *landsmaal,* or "New Norse," based on the old Norse dialects.

Two other factors complicate the tracing of Norwegian family names. Often the name of the farm on which a family lived was attached after the personal name. If Olaf Larson lived on a farm named "Bakken," his full name was Olaf Larson Bakken. In some regions the word *gard* or *gaard,* "farm," was part of the farm name, as in "Larsgard." If a family moved to a different farm, it substituted the name of the new farm for the name of the old one. Thus the farm name was not really a family name, but a name attached to the personal name to identify the person's home. This practice was generally abandoned late in the nineteenth century.

Migration to America complicated the situation even more, for the immigrants had to adopt a permanent, fixed family name to adapt to custom here. Most of them Americanized their patronymic name and used it as their surname, such as Johnson and Olson. There were so many people with names of that type, however, that other immigrants took the name of their farm or their locality at home or an entirely new name.

Paternal Ancestors 24

Anders Aadneson was Gladys' great-great-great-great-great grandfather. He lived on the tenant farm Sva, which was on the farm Natvik. He married Martha Sjursdatter in 1712. One of their three children was Roland Andersen (b. 1720), who married Catharina Jorgensdatter; they, too, lived at Natvik. This couple had two children, one of whom was Anna.

Anna Rolandsdatter Natvik married Erik Halvorsen Hovland in 1773. Erik's father, Halvor Krogen, lived in Outer Kroken, Norway. Erik had been baptized in 1742 on the 17th Sunday after Trinity by the pastor of Hafslo. After Erik was confirmed in the church, he went to

Aardalstangen and worked as a farm hand on the farm Laegreid. When he married Anna, they built and lived in the tenant farm Hola which they founded on the farm Hovland.

The farms Natvik and Hovland are important for our history because they are usually regarded as the places where the Windedahl family history begins. One of Norway's many coves is Natvik (other spellings: Nadvik, Naddvik), located on the south bank of Aardalsfjord, at the east end of the Sognefjord. The Natvik valley in the cove is divided into two parts by a stream called Nysetelv (Nyset River), namely, the Hovland farm on the east and the Natvik farm on the west. Today about a half-dozen tenant farms are on each of these two main farms, but in the mid-1800s there were about twice as many.

Jorgen Erikson Natvik (1794-1889) and Helvik Frederikke Andreasdatter Bakken (1797-1890) were Gladys' great-great grandparents. Jorgen, Erik and Anna's eighth child, married Helvik in 1816. She was living on the tenant farm Bakken in Natvik. Working in the woods to cut logs for the local sawmill was one of the few cash-paying jobs available around Natvik. Jorgen had such a job. One winter, while sitting drinking with his brother-in-law Ole, Jorgen traded his job for Ole's lease on the tenant farm Sva in Natvik. Afterwards Ole regretted that he had made the trade. Jorgen and Helvik moved to Sva and had twelve children, six of whom eventually emigrated to the United States. While working in the woods, Jorgen accidentally killed his son Ola, 13 years old. Jorgen lived to be 94 and Helvik died at 93.

Metta Jorgensdatter Natvik (later Vindedal) (1832-1916) and Andreas Johannesson Ofredal (later Vindedal) (date?) were Gladys' great-grandparents. In 1851 Jorgen and Helvik's daughter Metta married Andreas Johannesson, who lived on a farm at Ofredal, west of Aardal. They were married at Natvik, but sometime thereafter they rented the tenant farm Vindedal ("winding valley") in the Vindedalen valley west of Laerdal. In 1868 three of their children (John, Helen, and Belle) emigrated to southern Wisconsin. They sent home money that they had earned, which enabled their parents and the other five children to join them in Wisconsin four years later. Andreas then took the name of their former farm home, Vindedal, as the family name, but used a more fashionable spelling, Windedahl. His oldest son, John, made the same change, but his younger sons, who settled in Minnesota, streamlined the name to Windahl. In the United States Metta was called Mattie.

Why did so many Norwegians emigrate to the United States in the nineteenth century, especially from central Norway? The socioeconomic situation was the primary factor. Norway was essentially an agricultural country, yet it had so little farmland. Ownership of a farm passed from the farm owner to his oldest son. The daughters and younger sons did not inherit the farm, and land was seldom available anywhere for purchase. As for the tenant farmer, he could transfer the lease to his house to one of his children, but that son or daughter could hardly eke out a living from the bit of land on which the house was built.

Jobs were scarce, and the large size of the families added to the problem. Thus economic survival was extremely difficult for many Norwegians. After some persons had emigrated, many of their relatives and friends at home were eager to join them. The trip across the Atlantic was arduous, for there was often a shortage of food and drinking water, and sometimes there was disease. The conditions were not so miserable as those confronting the Palatine Germans a century and a half earlier, however, for most of the Norwegian emigrants survived.

When Metta and Andreas sailed to America with five of their children in 1872, the voyage took fourteen weeks. They landed at Quebec City, then proceeded up the St. Lawrence River and across four of the Great Lakes to Milwaukee. They journeyed, probably by team and wagon, to Sun Prairie, Wisconsin. Two years later they moved on to Spring Valley, Minnesota. Andreas died in middle age, and Metta moved to the Dakota Territory, locating near the present town of Oldham, South Dakota. Several of her children lived in that area too.

John Andrew Windedahl (1851-1916) and Johanna Hanson (1847-1892) were Gladys' grandparents. John, the oldest of the children of Metta and Andreas, married--probably in Sun Prairie--Johanna Hanson from Norway in 1872, the same year that his parents arrived from the homeland with their five youngest children. After living at Sun Prairie for two years, they moved with the rest of the family to Spring Valley. In 1879 John moved with his family to Lake County in Dakota

Territory where he filed on a homestead. He bought a team of oxen, but had to mortgage the farm to pay for it. Unable to make the payments because of crop failure and lack of sufficient farm implements, he lost the farm through foreclosure of the mortgage. In 1882 the family moved west into Miner County, where John had filed on both a tree claim and a preemption, each consisting of one hundred sixty acres.[25] He had built a sod house there before bringing out the family. After four years he built a small frame house, hauling the lumber by oxen and wagon from the county seat, Howard, twenty-one miles away. The Redstone Creek ran through a corner of the farm, providing water for the livestock. Buffalo and cow chips and tightly twisted grass hay provided fuel for the home.

In 1883 Frank Ward arrived from Carthage, New York, representing the Western Townsite Company, which purchased John's preemption for $200. The purchase gave rights to the new railroad to cross the land. In addition, Western Townsite sent in surveyors who platted on the preemption a new town, which was named Carthage after the town in New York.

On January 12, 1888, a great blizzard struck Carthage, and pupils and teachers were snowbound in the schoolhouse. "The wind was blowing so hard and the air was so full of snow that you could not see your own hand held up in front of your face," wrote John and Johanna's son Carl years later. The fathers of the children obtained rope from Dickson's hardware store and tied one end to the store. Next they strung out the rope to the school, three blocks away, and tied the other end of the rope to it. Then, instructing the pupils and teachers to hold on to the rope, the men conducted them to the store. The children spent the night on the upstairs floor of stores and in some homes. Storekeepers exhausted their supply of blankets, which were wrapped around the children to protect them from the bitter cold. "Many people lost their lives in that blizzard; some within a few feet of their own house which they could not find; some froze their feet so badly that they had to be amputated" (Carl Windedahl).

John and Johanna lived on their tree claim at the edge of town and operated it as a successful farm. Eventually he established a profitable dealership in "Farm Implements, Wagons and Buggies" in Carthage.

When the "Norwegian Evangelical Lutheran Church" was founded in Carthage, John was a charter member. In those days the Norwegian Lutheran churches generally disapproved of lodges, and John eventually belonged to several lodges. Finally some members of the local church went to Pastor Bongsto and complained, "We don't think it is right for John to be both a treasurer in a lodge and the treasurer of our church. We think that you should go and speak to him about it." So the pastor did. John replied, "When the churches take care of the widows and orphans [which the lodges were doing], then we won't need the lodges. Until then, I am going to serve the lodges too." The minister was satisfied, and John continued as treasurer in both organizations.

Johanna and John had eight children, but two daughters died from diphtheria. Johanna was not in good health and died in 1892. John died accidentally in 1916 when he was working alone in the Farmers' (grain) Elevator in Carthage. He evidently went up to the top of the shaft, slipped, and fell to the floor far below.

Maternal Ancestors

Ole Guttormson and Gunild Knudsdatter were Gladys' great grandparents. Presumably Ole was born on the family farm about fifteen miles south of Geilo; the place still bears the name Guttormsgard. Gunild, born in 1808, was from Imingeiet, the present-day Imingen, about 22 miles farther south. Gladys has her wood chest bearing her name and the place and date of birth. The couple lived at Guttormsgard, where their nine children were born. In 1857 they emigrated with eight of their children, including son Ola, to Clayton County in northeastern Iowa.

1857 was the year of the great Norwegian immigration into Clayton County. The McGregor (Iowa) newspaper, *The Times,* reported: "On Saturday last the Northern Belle [a riverboat on the Mississippi] delivered at McGregor nearly 100 immigrants from Norway. . . . very few of the company looked to be over 35 or 40 years of age. Boxes, wooden trunks and cases of all shapes and sizes, strongly banded with iron, painted and marked with hieroglyphics to us undecipherable, were carried from the boat in the levee until the wharf and road for several rods were completely blocked up. The appearance of some of the wooden trunks was very ancient, one of them we saw was marked 1707. . . The Norwegians are a most valuable accession to the state."26

Ola Embrikkson Nestegard (later Larsgard) (1801-1866) and Ingeborg Olsdatter Bakkegard (1801-1893) were also Gladys' great-grandparents. Ingeborg's parents were Ole Pukerud (b. 1774) and Guri Svensdatter, who bought a farm called Bakkegard around 1800. Judging from a published report 27 we have a bit of a skeleton in the closet when we come to Ingeborg. She and Ola Embrikkson Nestegard were engaged, but they plotted to get possession of the Larsgard farm, which belonged to an old man, Ola Knutson Larsgard, a widower. In 1826 she "fooled" him into marrying her. The next year she gave birth to a son, Ola Olson Larsgard, and her husband died. Less than a year later she married the man she really loved, Ola Embrikkson Nestegard, and he moved in with her on the farm. He followed custom by replacing his old farm name, Nestegard, with his new one, Larsgard. This arrangement was quite successful for the couple until young Ola Olson became an adult. Then he asserted his legal right to ownership and forced his mother and step-father to move out. Therefore in 1857 Ingeborg, her second husband, and four of their children emigrated to Clayton County, Iowa; one of the children was daughter Borghild. Their other four children remained in Norway. The Guttormson and Larsgard families became acquainted on shipboard when they crossed the Atlantic together, and both settled in the same county. Gladys has a small, handmade wooden case which the Larsgards brought with them, probably filled with butter. In America Ola and Ingeborg Larsgard retained the farm name as their family name, spelling it in the Dano-Norwegian manner, Larsgaard. He is reported to have died in a drunken brawl.

Ola Guttormson was fifteen and Borghild Larsgard was thirteen when they got acquainted on shipboard. Their parents evidently became close friends in Iowa, and as these two children grew up, a romance developed. He joined the Union Army during the Civil War; his experiences included taking care of General Grant's horses and participating in General Sherman's "march to the sea." Some accounts indicate that Borghild worked in some American homes during the war and that the experience fostered her knowledge of the English language. Ola probably knew that she would wait for him until the war was over, and in 1866 they were married by the Justice of the Peace in Elkader, the county seat of Clayton County.

Sometime after arrival in America, Ola Guttormson changed his name to Ole Gutterson (Ola would sound feminine to Americans), while his brother Peder changed to Peter Getterson. Borghild changed hers to Betsy Olson and her sister Sunnev became Susan Olson. Girls invariably followed the American custom of using the masculine form such as Olson rather than the Norwegian feminine form such as Olsdatter. Eventually Borghild returned to her Norwegian forename.

Before 1872 the young couple moved to Sioux County in western Iowa, for records show that Susan was married that year in the Gutterson home in Sioux County. In 1854 Ole and Betsy moved to South Dakota, where he had secured a homestead and a tree claim eleven miles from Carthage. They had five daughters, one of whom was Gusta Martha.

Ole, like John Windedahl, was a founder of the Norwegian Lutheran church in Carthage. According to custom, only the men were listed as the charter members; wives and children were taken for granted. For four years (1908-1912) the Carthage Norwegian Lutheran Church was served every third Sunday by the Reverend P. E. Bongsto, pastor of the Norwegian Lutheran church in Woonsocket, thirty-seven miles away. Making the long journey by horse and buggy, he stayed overnight at the Ole Gutterson home on his way to and from Carthage. The Guttersons moved from their farm into Carthage in 1914 when they traded the farm for a house which Gladys' parents had built.

After settling in the United States, Gladys' ancestors, both maternal and paternal, remained in the Lutheran tradition. Grandfather Windedahl, as we have seen, displayed some independence of thought in regard to churches versus lodges.

7

GLADYS AND HER PARENTS

Gladys was the daughter of Henry Olai Windedahl (1877-1940) and Gusta Martha Gutterson (1883-1970). Henry, son of John and Johanna Windedahl, was born in Spring Valley, Minnesota, and attended elementary school in Carthage, South Dakota, after his parents moved there. His mother was ill much of the time and he helped her with the housework. She died when he was fifteen years old. Young Henry was especially interested in learning, a fact observed by his father and by the pastor of his church. Therefore those two men arranged for Henry to enroll in the "Prep Department" of Augsburg College in Minneapolis. The pastor, like other pastors at that time, was eager to direct young men into the Christian ministry. After he had enrolled, Henry found, to his dismay, that all his schoolmates were preparing to become ministers. That was not his goal, so he quit school at the end of his first academic year, 1899-1900.

The following autumn Henry registered at South Dakota Agricultural College at Brookings, which he attended for two years. His report cards, which Gladys possesses, show that his courses included civil government, U.S. history, typewriting, arithmetic, and bookkeeping. When he was young he played the "fiddle" at country dances, and later he taught Gladys how to dance.

As a result of the large families, there were many young people at Carthage who socialized at school, church, picnics, and dances. Youth of Norwegian descent tended to associate with each other more than with the youth of Swedish and German descent. The reasons were that nearly all of them attended the Norwegian church and they had a common language and cultural background. The youth of the Gutterson and Windedahl families, as Norwegian Americans, became close friends. By 1901 Martha Gutterson was "going with" Carl Windedahl, one of Henry's three brothers. When Henry came home from college in December 1901, he attended the wedding dance of his brother Chris. At the dance, which was held in the home of the brothers' father, Martha and Henry first became "interested" in each other. This dance changed the course of their lives. Carl had to find another girl.

Henry worked in Huron, South Dakota, in 1903, part of the time for the railroad and part of the time as a day laborer in town for $2 per day. He wrote letters to Martha describing the fellowship he enjoyed as a member of the Odd Fellows lodge there, which held meetings each Monday night. In one letter he reported that on a Friday night the I.O.O.F. and its women's auxiliary, the Rebekahs, "had a sociable. We had a good supper there and danced till about one o'clock and we had a fine time." On Sunday the two groups met at the lodge hall and then marched to church together (probably not a Lutheran church). Henry also went at times to "hear the Starvation Army or what most people call the Salvation Army." Nevertheless, he longed for the country, and in the summer he left to work in the harvest. Next he returned to Carthage where he and his brother Carl went into partnership in both farming and well drilling.

Meanwhile Martha clerked in the general store of her brother-in-law, Thomas Strand, in Carthage, but that ended when the store burned down. Later she moved to Fairview, South Dakota, and worked in the general store of her cousin, Henry Getterson, who had changed the spelling of his name.

By summer 1906 Martha and Henry had decided on marriage, but accomplishing it was not easy. The plans had to be made by correspondence, and money was scarce. Besides, he had a special problem. He and his neighbors were exchanging work in threshing grain, but he had expected that the harvesting would be finished before the wedding. Heavy rains, however, had delayed the threshing that autumn. With the unpredictability of the weather, poor Henry was not even sure he could attend his own wedding! Two days before the date, he wrote this to Martha:

> They thought it was too wet and soft in the field [to thresh at his farm] . . . I will have to go and see Bailey [evidently the owner of the threshing machine] . . . I think that he will get through at Strand's today and then he is going to Stratton's and I suppose I will have to go there tomorrow so I have to be a threshing anyway.

Well, are you ready? I am not but am going to be anyway. We have got to get through with this now some way. If we wait till I get ready I don't think it will ever be.

In spite of the odds, they made it. On November 14, 1906, they became husband and wife in the home of the Lutheran pastor in Howard, the county seat, where they obtained their license. After they were married, their first home was about two miles southwest of Carthage, on the farm owned in partnership with brother Carl. There Gladys was born on August 22, 1907.

At the age of three Gladys displayed her roaming Viking instincts when she, with her dog Fido, wandered off into a wheat field. There she lay down and took her afternoon nap, hidden from view by the tall grain. Her alarmed mother searched for her, fearing that she might have fallen into the nearby creek or might be playing in a wolf's hole, or nest, along the creek bank. Calling out Gladys' name and Fido's name as she went, she found Fido barking and jumping up and down so that he could be seen above the heads of grain. Faithful Fido continued to guard Gladys until her mother arrived.

From 1912 to 1914 the pastor of the Norwegian Lutheran Churches in Carthage and the town of Howard was the Reverend P. E. Moen. On the weekends that he came to Carthage, his wife and daughter Emerentia usually came with him and stayed overnight with Gladys' parents. Emerentia and Gladys played

together. Once Emerentia hit Gladys while trying
to get her out of bed in the morning, and Gladys
hit back. Emerentia ran crying to her parents,
saying, "Gladys hit me!" When she started to return, her parents asked, "Why do you want to go
back to Gladys if she hit you?" She said, "She
won't hit me if I don't hit her first!"

In general, Norwegian Americans adapted
rather quickly to American customs; they wanted
to fit in, to be like other Americans.
Nevertheless, some preferred their ethnic heritage, but as with other ethnic groups, adherence
to the old ways created problems in language and
religion. Often those two types of problems were
combined.

In Carthage the Norwegian Lutheran
Church followed the European custom in which
the men sat on the right side of the church and the
women on the left during the services. Around
1913 Gladys' mother and another lady deliberately broke the custom by sitting beside their hus-
bands one Sunday. Gladys and the daughter of the
other couple sat with their parents and giggled,
enjoying the surprised expressions of friends. In
succeeding months the other women gradually
changed to the new pattern too.

Virtually none of the Norwegian immigrants knew English when they arrived, and some
never learned much of it. Their church services
were conducted in Norwegian for many years.
This was the case in Carthage until 1927, when
the congregation decided that two-thirds of the
services should be in English. When in 1931 the
Reverend J. E. Borgen became the part-time pas-

tor, preaching alternate Sundays in De Smet and in Carthage, he conducted all his regular services in English. For the benefit of the old-timers in the church, he voluntarily held an additional service in Norwegian in the afternoon. "Without these pioneers," he said, "we would not have had a church."

On the national scene in America, the United Norwegian Church, the Norwegian Synod, and the Hauge Synod merged in 1917 to form the Evangelical Lutheran Church. At its first biennial convention, held in Fargo, North Dakota, in 1918, the delegates decided to drop the word "Norwegian" from the denominational name, partly because they wished to demonstrate in wartime that they were loyal Americans, not foreigners. This action aroused such a storm of conservative protest within the churches that it was not until 1946 that "Evangelical" was substituted for "Norwegian" in the name. The Carthage church retained its original name, Norwegian Evangelical Lutheran Church.

The Carthage Lutheran church obtained, temporarily, its first resident, full-time pastor in 1921. Previously services were conducted only once or twice a month by a Norwegian Lutheran minister from another town. The Christian Church in Carthage, however, had a full-time minister and therefore had a Sunday school. Gladys had playmates who attended the Sunday school, so she went too. Thus began her ecumenical attitude.

A traveling evangelist conducted some revival meetings at the Christian Church and remarked that the Congregational Church in town was "tearing the Bible to pieces and throwing it in the wastebasket!" When this was reported to Gladys' mother, she strongly objected to his statement, for she believed in honesty and tolerance. This attitude was part of her philosophy of life, which made a powerful impression on Gladys.

Some tension existed between the Norwegian and Swedish Lutheran churches in town, a heritage from the European background. But the influence of World War II and economic factors caused the two churches to merge in 1947 to form the Trinity Lutheran Church. Physical union of the buildings was accomplished to some extent by moving one wing of the Norwegian church and attaching it at a right angle to the side of the Swedish church. Many of the Norwegians lamented the loss of their church, and at the time of the consolidation one of Gladys' uncles vowed, "I'm not going to any Swedish church!" His wife remarked about the union, "It just doesn't seem right, but the young folks seem to get along all right."

The years 1918-1927 were prosperous ones for Henry and Martha, and Gladys was able to attend Augustana College in Sioux Falls for two years, 1924-26, where she earned a teaching certificate. Next she taught in a one-room country school, Afton No. 2 in Sanborn County, a school which both she and her mother before her had attended.

In contrast to the previous ten years, the next decade was very strenuous for the family. Gladys did not like teaching and was not sure

what she wanted to do. She returned to
Augustana for a term, clerked in a general store
in Carthage for a year and a half, then returned to
Augustana again. In 1929 her father's health
failed and he became very depressed. Gladys left
college again and worked in the general store
once more, but the next year it failed. To give
her father a psychological change, the family
lived in various places in South Dakota, including
Hot Springs, but the effort to restore Henry's
health was in vain. Gladys' young brother
George (born 1921) attended one elementary
school after another. The family moved to Sioux
Falls in 1931 and operated a small lunchroom
near the Augustana campus. Here Gladys dated
her first serious "boyfriend;" she called off the
engagement after she realized that they did not
have enough in common (luckily for me!).
Gladys returned to teaching a country school in
the Carthage area in 1932.

Martha's sister Jennie with her husband
Thomas Strand and family had moved to Oregon
in the 1920s. They encouraged the Windedahls to
move there too, and in 1933 Gladys went to
Oregon to investigate. Cousin Thelma Strand
found a temporary job for her in the Woolworth
store in Salem where she herself worked. The
next summer Gladys returned to Carthage and
helped the rest of her family move to Salem,
where they bought a house on Fairview Avenue.
The house was on a one-acre plot which produced
fruit and vegetables, an important feature in the
1930s. Jobs were scarce, but Gladys' mother
found work as a housekeeper for a lady next door
who was in her late 90s. In addition to the Great

Depression, the family had to cope with Henry's illness; he helped by taking care of the yard and garden.

After working in the Woolworth store again, Gladys enrolled at the University of Oregon with only ten dollars in her purse. While there she lived in a student cooperative, serving as senior resident for the other girls, who were younger. She was on the honor roll, and by majoring in education she was qualified to teach in Oregon public schools when she graduated. Next she taught English in the high school in the town of Condon in eastern Oregon for a year (1937-38). Once again she found that she did not enjoy teaching, and because of her father's illness, she wanted to live nearer home. Therefore she returned to Salem and worked at the information desk in the Oregon State Library for a year and a half. Next, she was office manager in the Oregon State Department of Education for nearly three years. In December 1940 her father died at the age of 63.

In the fall of 1942 Gladys enlisted in the Women's Army Auxiliary Corps and for a year recruited for it in Wisconsin and Upper Michigan. When it was replaced by the Women's Army Corps, she did not reenlist, but attended the University of Wisconsin in Madison and received her graduate library degree in 1944. Some lasting friendships were formed with her classmates. On the same day that she received a letter from Oregon stating that the offer of a library position had to be withdrawn for lack of funds, she received a letter from J. C. K. Preus inviting her--for the second time--to become the Educational and Editorial Assistant in the Education Office of the Norwegian Lutheran Church in Minneapolis. She accepted the offer and assisted in the promotion of the denomination's educational program. In the fall she collected material for Dr. Preus's illustrated article on stained glass windows in the 1944 issue of the church's popular annual, *Christmas.* In the spring she traveled for the Education Office and gave talks on matters pertaining to parish education and higher education at district conventions of the various organizations of the Norwegian Lutheran Church. Gladys' mother lived with her in both Madison and Minneapolis and worked in a hospital in both cities. A month before Gladys began work in Minneapolis, the Norwegian Lutheran Church of America voted at its biennial conference to change its name to the Evangelical Lutheran Church; the change became official in 1946.

Gladys still preferred librarianship, however, so after a year she accepted an offer to become Head of Circulation in the Oregon State Library in Salem in 1945. The following year she became the Cataloger in the Salem Public Library where Hugh Morrow was the Librarian. He was a congenial man, and I remember that when he learned that I was interested in the history of religion, he showed me the library's set of Sir James G. Frazer's *The Golden Bough,* a detailed study of ancient religion. In Salem Gladys and her mother were members of St. Mark's Lutheran Church, which belonged to the United Lutheran Church.

In 1946 Gladys and her mother bought a large house on the corner of Court and Twelfth

Streets, near the Willamette University campus. Using the house as a dormitory, they rented rooms to Willamette male students.

Both Gladys and her parents lived their religion quietly rather than preached it. They had no conversion experience, and none was expected in their Lutheran churches. While Gladys was in high school her closest friend was Marian Raesly, who was not a church member nor even religious in the customary sense of the term. Thus early in life Gladys began to judge people on the basis of their character and personality, not their religion. This made her more tolerant of the diversity of religious views, including those of her future husband.

Now we turn to our married life.

8

MARRIAGE AND GRADUATE STUDY

After our honeymoon Gladys and I lived in one of my mother's apartments for a month, and then began our nine-month trip to libraries to learn more about Christian beginnings. By this time I had read virtually all the books pertaining to the subject in Oregon libraries; the next step was to search in larger libraries. I had inherited $6,000 from my father, and with that to finance us, we set forth. On December 17, 1947 we removed the rear seat of our sedan, loaded that area and the trunk, and headed for California. Looking for specific books in the extensive bibliography I had compiled as well as for additional titles, we examined the card catalogs in various libraries. At the Pacific School of Religion in Berkeley we used its excellent library and enjoyed the Palestine Institute Museum. I had a fruitful conference there with Professor McCown, whose book, *The Search for the Real Jesus,* had strongly impressed me.

Churches, museums, and religious sites were also of interest to us, for we wanted to learn all we could about religion, past and present. In San Francisco we saw the Dolores Spanish Mission. A postcard we purchased lists 21 missions that have been preserved in southern California; the majority of them date from the last quarter of the eighteenth century.

After a brief stop at Stanford University, we drove on to Los Angeles, passing many roadside stands selling citrus fruit and olives. I was very fond of ripe olives, so I bought a gallon can of small ones for $1.65. By the time we finished eating them, several weeks later, I was so tired of them that I never ate another for many years.

In Los Angeles we rented a room for the month of January. At the University of Southern California we used the library and I conferred with Eric Titus, a professor of New Testament. We borrowed books from the Los Angeles Public Library. Sitting at a picnic table in Exposition Park, I read books while Gladys copied passages from them on our portable Remington typewriter which we had brought with us. In the Los Angeles Public Library we found a large rack full of trashy religious journals, prominently displayed in the room. I asked the librarian in the Religion and Psychology room if the library subscribed to those journals. She replied, "We subscribe to the standard ones, but this ephemeral stuff [motioning toward the rack] is given to us, or we wouldn't have it around!" In one magazine the eccentric group that published it listed the names of many prominent persons who had spoken at its meetings. One name was that of Edgar J. Goodspeed, the famous New Testament translator and scholar. After I returned home, I wrote to him to ask if he had really spoken to those people and if he agreed with their ideas, as they implied. He replied that he did not agree with

them, but it was his practice to speak to all kinds
of groups if invited. This incident illustrates the
name-dropping tactic used by some religious pro-
pagandists to imply falsely that famous people
agree with them.

In Los Angeles we found an abundance of
odd religious groups to visit. One of them was
the International Church of the Foursquare
Gospel, founded by Aimee Semple McPherson.
Aimee was deceased, but the ministry in the
church, the Angelus Temple, was being continued
by her son and daughter-in-law, Ralph and Lorna
McPherson, and by a male convert (I failed to
record his name). Arriving early, we attended one
of their Sunday evening services. A member of
the church sat down beside me and asked if I
thought the Lord was coming soon. "No, I don't
think so," I replied. He responded, "Oh, I do. I
feel it; I feel it!" By the time the service was
over, we realized why he felt it. The preliminar-
ies of the service were intended to provide an im-
pressive show, and indeed they did. A band in
red and blue uniforms played loudly. A choir,
dressed in white, was located high above the plat-
form, half on each side of it. The two sides of the
choir took turns at descending stairs to the plat-
form to sing, and as each group sang, spotlights
with rotating color filters shone upon it.

The convert co-leader preached the sermon,
using Daniel 2 and Ezekiel 38 as texts. He concentrated on verses 14-16 in Ezekiel, according to
which the Lord God prophesies that God will
come down from the north with a mighty army
and attack Israel. The preacher interpreted the
passage as prophecy that in 1950 Russian soldiers

would march into Palestine and kill all the Jews; next, the Russians would fight among themselves; then God would send hailstones and kill all the Russian soldiers in Palestine. At the same time the Russians would attack Alaska; this notion was based on the preacher's recent trip to Alaska where he said he saw American preparations for war. And then, he predicted, Hallelujah, the Lord will come! The preacher concluded with an emotional appeal to the audience to accept the Lord as their Savior immediately, before it was too late, and to ask the preacher to pray for them. The hymns sung that evening were generally emotional ones about heaven and the Lord's coming. The church also held a meeting in the middle of each week that was devoted to "divine healing." In the service of the Bible Institute of Los Angeles (BIOLA) also the dominant theme was "the Lord is coming soon." Gladys and I were shocked by the extent to which fear of atomic bombs and of war with the Soviet Union was being used by fundamentalist churches to scare people into joining.

In the services we attended, both the Unity church and the Institute of Religious Science emphasized prayer, God's Spirit, and spiritual healing. Both used the term "truth" frequently in a metaphysical rather than a scientific sense. In sharp contrast to those churches, the Ethical Culture Society discussed the ethics and philosophy of prominent writers and philosophers, past and current; the addresses were delivered by Dr. Arthur E. Briggs. We also visited several Methodist and Lutheran churches in which the sermons were quite traditional. The First Congregational Church had a progressive feature:

a School of Religion that offered factual courses on religion four days a week.

Gladys saw among the church listings in a newspaper the notice of the First Unitarian Church of Los Angeles. I had not heard of the Unitarians before, but Gladys said she believed that they were closer to my views than any other church. Therefore we attended a Sunday service of that church and heard the minister, Reverend Stephen H. Fritchman, preach on "The Progressive and His Church." I was impressed with the sensible approach to religion. Afterwards we had a conference with him, and he gave us leaflets and a copy of his book, *Men of Liberty,* consisting of biographical sketches of religious liberals from Michael Servetus to Theodore Parker.

The Huntington Library and Art Gallery at San Marino was another stop. Its collection of art, manuscripts, and rare books excels in quantity and quality. One evening at Van Nuys we saw the first public showing of a new automobile, the Davis, with two wheels in the rear and only one in the front. Unfortunately for the manufacturer, the car broke down in the middle of the exhibition.

Then on to Phoenix, where we rented a room in a private home for three weeks in February. We began to organize and blend together the material that we had collected and that I had gathered before marriage. As usual, we did some sight-seeing, and Reg Manning's *Cartoon Guide of Arizona* was a delight to use. The abundance of Indian names amused us, and I inflicted on my new wife puns such as "Let Navaho the corn, while you Yavapai."

While driving along a highway in Arizona we stopped at a gift shop that featured pottery made by Indians in a nearby reservation. The trader, or storekeeper, showed us a plate which lacked the beautiful painted decoration that was on the other plates. He explained that the girl who had made it had broken a tribal law and that the medicine man had decreed that as punishment she could use only a simple scratched pattern as decoration. Later I wished that we had purchased it as an illustration of religious authoritarianism, which has been all too common throughout history.

On our trip we read of an amusing incident that occurred at an Indian trading post. A woman in the reservation made rugs which the post sold to tourists. One day she gave the trader a welcome doormat which she had made for him. Across its middle the letters H E L L were woven. Pointing to the letters, he asked, "What's this?" She replied, "Says 'Hello." He asked, "Where's the O?" She answered, "No room for the O." The moral of this incident, of course, is that hell results when people fail to plan ahead!

We continued to visit various churches. In the regular Sunday service at the First Congregational Church in Phoenix the minister called upon the congregation to confess its sins, based on 1 John 1:8-9: "If we say we have no sin, we deceive ourselves, and the truth is not in us. If we confess our sins, . . . he will forgive our sins and cleanse us from all unrighteousness." The congregation recited in unison the Confession of

Sin, and then the minister commanded it to "Go and sin no more." But when the routine was repeated the next Sunday, the whole congregation was again regarded as sinners! I wondered, "Does the minister assume that, after all, no one has really been cleansed from sin, or does he assume that no one heeded his advice to 'sin no more'?"

To save money we moved to a cabin in the Mountain Club area near Prescott in northern Arizona. The forested mountains there contrast sharply with the deserts of southern Arizona. Naturally we took a trip to the Grand Canyon. In ten weeks we completed the organization of the information we had gathered and on May 10 began the drive to Chicago.

I was attracted to the University of Chicago because some of the best books I had read were written by some of its professors: Edgar J. Goodspeed, Shirley Jackson Case, Harold R. Willoughby, and Donald W. Riddle. We rented an apartment near the campus, and I used several of the university's libraries. In the summer quarter I enrolled for two courses, classical Greek and "Paul: The Man and His Message." The latter was taught by Paul Schubert, visiting from Yale University. Gladys and I were fascinated by the university's multitude of free public lectures delivered by experts. Gladys worked in the library of the university's School of Education. We continued to visit all types of churches, ranging from the Moody Bible Institute to the First Unitarian Church.

By this time I had decided that writing books on religion should be my vocation. I visited Professor Riddle to ask for advice. He told me that I had the right attitude to become a scholar, but he warned that it is virtually impossible to earn a living from writing scholarly books. He said that scholarly manuscripts either are not published or else do not sell enough copies to be profitable. He added that he had a good manuscript lying on a shelf, with no publisher for it. At the close of the summer quarter I had a conference with Professor Schubert, and he urged me to get a Ph.D. at the University of Chicago. He said, "This is one of the best schools in the country, and it shares your zeal for research on religion." Nevertheless, in spite of Riddle's warning, I said, "No, I want to write books."

After driving back to Oregon, we lived in an apartment in Gladys' mother's home. Using a room in my mother's house as an office, I began to write a manuscript reporting what I had learned about the beginning of Christianity. Gladys worked in the Salem Public Library.

In January 1949 I interviewed the Reverend Brooks Moore, minister of the First Methodist Church in Salem. Concerning the Youth for Christ movement founded by Billy Graham, he said: "We tried to cooperate with them, but we found it wasn't possible. They wanted all the marbles to roll their way!" Concerning the Salem Ministerial Association, he reported that conservative ministers dominated it and that the pastor of the First Baptist Church had obtained the office of president of the association by using unethical tactics. He said that the liberal ministers were organizing a Religious Council with both lay and clerical members, a council which would be too large for the conservatives to control. Concerning the teaching of Bible in public schools after school hours, a procedure then being tested in Salem, he said that the course used was produced by a good organization, the International Council of Religious Education, but the teachers evidently put their own interpretation on it. (He was certainly right, for I visited one of the classes and heard the fundamentalist teacher assert, in fundamentalist fashion, that the Creation story is literal history). Reverend Moore commented: "We have a hard time working with them [fundamentalists] for a few weeks of Vacation Bible school, so how can we expect to cooperate on a nine-months course in public schools?"

I showed my mother some Jewish literature written at the time of the beginning of Christianity, and I explained how some of the ideas in it influenced the New Testament. Mother was favorably impressed and remarked, "Anyone should be able to see that you are trying to get to the bottom of things." We had seldom discussed details of my studies because they were complex. Now I was glad to see that she, too, was willing to learn unorthodox knowledge. I will always cherish the memory of that conversation, which we had only a few months before she died at the age of 71.

In the autumn of 1949 Gladys read a newspaper item which stated that a representative of the American Unitarian Association in Boston, Reverend Lon Call, would be in a room in the Senator Hotel on a certain evening, and that anyone interested in organizing a Unitarian Fellowship was invited to meet with him. I went, at Gladys' suggestion. Ten of us, the minimum number to form a "Fellowship," attended a second meeting; we organized and I was elected president. The Fellowship met Sunday evenings in the basement of the YWCA; in less than a year we had thirty members.

The experience with the Salem Unitarian Fellowship convinced me that I should become a Unitarian minister. In July 1950 Gladys and I drove to Chicago where I had a conference with Dr. Robbins, the president of Meadville Theological Seminary, a Unitarian school included in the Federated Theological Faculty arrangement at the University of Chicago. I filled out the application for admission in the fall, and Robbins asked me to give the name of a Unitarian minister as a reference. I wrote down the name of the only Unitarian minister I knew (slightly), the young minister of the Unitarian church in Eugene, Oregon. Gladys investigated the outlook for a library position for herself on the campus. We found that rental housing was scarce and inferior, for conditions had deteriorated during the war. Consequently, we purchased a co-op apartment on Woodlawn Avenue, near the campus and across the street from St. Thomas Catholic Church.

We returned to Salem, but in September rented the house we had bought in West Salem and moved to our apartment in Chicago. I took the entrance examination required by the university and the Federated Theological Faculty. My score was B, except A on the biology section and

F on the art and architecture section. In the latter
section I was asked to name all the parts of the
interior of a cathedral shown in a drawing. I had
not even a hazy idea of the names, for I had never
studied the subject or even been inside a cathedral! To our astonishment, Robbins rejected my
application, pointing to the F in art. Afterwards
the young minister in Eugene told me that his
name was the wrong one to give as a reference
because when he was a student at Meadville, he
had had a bitter disagreement with Robbins.

The rejection was a jolt to us, and I thought
we should move back to Oregon. But Gladys
searched through the catalogs of the University of
Chicago and found the Ph.D. program of the New
Testament Department in the Humanities
Division. The department was established by
Edgar J. Goodspeed in 1892, when the university
was founded. Its program was a thorough historical approach, designed to produce professors and
scholars. The program began with the broad
historical background: ancient history, Greek and
Roman religion, classical Greek language, and the
archaeology of Greek and Roman cities. Next, it
moved to the Hebrew, Hellenistic Greek, French,
and German languages, to the historical environments of the Old and New Testaments, and to
early church history and literature; then came the
intensive study of the text of the Bible. Finally, a
year was required for the doctoral dissertation,
which had to be an exhaustive investigation of one
historical topic in the field. In contrast, the Ph.D.
in Bible through the Divinity School involved
pastoral studies instead of historical background
and a pastoral or theological topic instead of a

historical one in the dissertation. Gladys recommended that I apply for the New Testament Department's program. Remembering Professor Schubert's advice and again following Gladys' suggestion, I applied and was admitted to the program. We had stood at the crossroads, and my wife had persuaded me to make the decision that made my future career possible. In the pastorate, with only a B.D. degree, I would have had neither the time nor the training for historical research. Dr. Robbins' adverse decision proved to be a blessing in disguise.

While I was studying for my doctorate, Gladys worked in various jobs at the John Crerar Library. Located downtown, it later moved to the campus of Illinois Institute of Technology, and presently is at the University of Chicago. It was endowed in 1889 by John Crerar, a wealthy manufacturer of railway supplies. Originally it was a general library; the only limit to its scope was Mr. Crerar's stipulation that the library should not contain "any dirty French novels." Shortly before Gladys began working there, its board of directors had decided to limit the library to science, technology, and medicine. Eventually Gladys was put in charge of decataloging the books and journals that were not in those fields; these were sold to other libraries.

In the 1950s there was much racial prejudice in Chicago. The Librarian at John Crerar, Herman Henkle, however, was free from it; he was the first Librarian there to elevate black women workers from the stacks in the basement to the circulation desk where they could interact with the public. Gladys and a black typist, Mrs. Mabel Reynolds, became close friends.

In the autumn of 1950 I completed my manuscript, 400 pages in length, and then rewrote it, reducing it to 300 pages. I submitted it, in turn, to three publishers: Longmans Green, Macmillan, and Beacon Press. Each rejected it. Douglas Tyacke of the Editorial Department at Longmans Green wrote: "Our Board felt that we as trade publishers could not successfully promote such a scholarly work as yours in the general market." The rejections should have been expected, for these were prominent publishers, but I had no reputation as an authority on the subject, did not know Greek and Hebrew, and had taken no graduate courses in the biblical field. Nevertheless, I had collected much information which was very useful in the graduate study that followed.

In January 1951 I registered in the university. Considering all the independent studying I had done, I hoped to graduate in about three years, even though five or six years was the usual time. The study of foreign languages, which I disliked, was a major reason that I had to spend five years.

Historical biblical study is fascinating, and the library resources for it at the university were tremendous. Among its many libraries were those of the Oriental Institute (deals with Near East), Classics Department, and Divinity School; they have since been integrated into the Regenstein Graduate Library. With open stacks and open access to journals, the libraries invited browsing by students and professors alike. With the small classes, students became well acquainted with professors who were giants in their field. I remember fondly Raymond Bowman, who taught Hebrew in relation to its origins; Robert M. Grant, expert on the church fathers and gnosticism; Carl Kraeling, archaeologist and Director of the Oriental Institute; Ralph Marcus, expert on early Judaism; Merrill Parvis, expert on New Testament textual criticism; J. Coert Rylaarsdam, expert Old Testament scholar; Gertrude Smith, expert classical Greek scholar; Allen Wikgren, expert on Hellenistic Greek and the history of biblical interpretation; and Harold Willoughby, authority on Greek and Roman mystery religions. Kraeling especially demonstrated that a person can be both an excellent scholar and an excellent teacher.

The New Testament Club at the university was founded in 1892 by Professor Goodspeed. The name was a misnomer because, like the New Testament Department, its scope was everything pertaining to understanding the whole Bible and early Christian history. All graduate students and professors in the field were members, and a research paper was read and discussed at the monthly meetings.

Professor Wikgren recommended me for membership in the Society of Biblical Literature and Exegesis (SBL; "and Exegesis" was omitted after 1963), which is composed of biblical scholars, most of whom are professors. It was founded in 1880. In my graduate-student days the membership and the scope of the programs at the annual meetings were small, but now the annual meetings are held jointly with the American

Academy of Religion (scope: the whole field of religion) and the American Schools of Oriental Research (scope: Near Eastern archaeology), and one or two large hotels are needed.

Studying for the Ph.D. at Chicago involved one written examination after another. In addition to course exams, I had reading exams in French and German, qualifying exams on the historical background of the Bible, and five days of field exams covering the whole field. Finally, an oral one on my dissertation. The first four years were years of learning more of what the Biblical scholars already knew. In my fifth year the research for my dissertation finally enabled me to do what I had been longing to do for years, namely, conduct original research.

The topic of my dissertation was "The Mosaic Eschatological Prophet." I traced in Judaism and early Christianity the notion of the coming in "the last days" of a prophet like Moses. Jesus is regarded as that prophet in Acts 3:20-26. Professors Wikgren and Marcus were my advisors; Wikgren had suggested the topic to me because of its possible connection with the Dead Sea scrolls. The dissertation was published in the Monograph Series of the *Journal of Biblical Literature*.

Finally, in September 1955 I received my Ph.D. at the age of 43. I was older than some of my professors. Although earning a doctorate at the University of Chicago takes longer than at most universities, the time is well spent. Without that thorough training, I would never have been able to do the research that I have done. I will always be beholden to both my alma maters.

Herman Clark, the Willamette professor whose course had aroused my curiosity, congratulated me and wrote:

> Your field is one that interests me very much. I consider it a most important subject for investigation, and much good should come from it. The greatest difficulty I see is to get people in general to change any belief to harmonize with what they learn of newly discovered facts. The "inertia of the mass" is mighty. But truth will triumph.

During these Chicago years Gladys' mother stayed with us several summers. She was a congenial woman, with a good sense of humor. We all enjoyed the companionship, our picnics in the parks along Lake Michigan, and our sightseeing together. There were--and are--so many interesting things to see and do in and around Chicago.

In the summer of 1948 we had visited many churches, but in 1950 we joined the First Unitarian Church near the campus. Because intellectual freedom is basic in Unitarianism, there is a wide variety of belief among its members and clergy. (To a lesser degree, considerable variety exists within both Catholic and Protestant churches--more than is generally admitted.) First Church was a rather conservative Unitarian church, under the leadership of Dr. Leslie Pennington. The Sunday service was formal; parts of it came from Christian tradition, and parts of it were similar to existentialist thought. After two years there, we changed our membership to the liberal Third Unitarian Church on Chicago's West

Side, where Edwin Buehrer was the minister. Here I preached a sermon, "The Upward Way," one Sunday morning. Its thesis was that Unitarians should establish a national research organization to develop a program for liberal religion and to produce educational materials to support the program. I introduced the sermon by describing an incident in my undergraduate college days in Oregon.

One of my classmates was a student minister of a Congregational church in a small town. One day he asked me if I would preach in his church on a Sunday when he had to attend a meeting elsewhere. I told him I would be glad to do so, but I was afraid that I might not do as well as he usually did. He replied, "Howard, don't worry. Some good is bound to come from it. If you preach a good sermon, you will do the people a lot of good, but if you preach a poor one, you will do me a lot of good!" So today I am going to do Reverend Buehrer a lot of good.

Occasionally we attended the services at the campus church, Rockefeller Chapel, where some of the sermons were preached by famous clergymen who were visiting Chicago. In 1950 we had the good fortune to hear Harry Emerson Fosdick preach there. We also attended and enjoyed many of the Tuesday night lectures at the Chicago Sinai Congregation, a Reform Judaism synagogue. Each winter its congregation sponsored an excellent series of lectures by outstanding speakers, non-Jewish and Jewish. We appreciated the synagogue's intelligent and progressive approach to religion and the problems of society.

The number of applicants for academic positions in teaching Bible in the United States far exceeded the number of positions available. After World War II the large expansion of academic schools was not in the private ones, but in the public colleges and universities, few of which have departments of religion. Another cause of the surplus of applicants was, and still is, the fact that after a few years in the ministry, many young clergymen decide that they would rather teach than preach.

A few months before I graduated I was interviewed for a position teaching religion at Milwaukee-Downer College. The interview process was complex. In many colleges the applicant is interviewed by the dean and the department head and sometimes the professor who has been teaching the courses the successful applicant will teach. At Milwaukee-Downer, however, a whole day schedule had been set up wherein I was shuttled around to interviews with the librarian and selected members of the faculty, administration, and students, a few at a time. The purpose of the procedure was to insure good relations between the new professor and the rest of the school. Privately I wondered if the time-consuming process necessarily produces harmonious relations. I suspected that I would not get the position when a Catholic professor, who did not teach religion, denounced liberal Christianity when he interviewed me. When the administration later sent me a letter of rejection, the reason given was that

I was too scholarly to be a good teacher. That angered me, and I vowed that someday I would demonstrate that I could be both a good scholar and a good teacher, like Carl Kraeling. A scholar can even be a superior teacher because, having conducted research himself or herself, he or she can inspire and train students to investigate. A professor who is not a scholar can hardly transmit a skill he or she has not acquired.

That summer Gladys and I joined the St. James Methodist Church a few blocks north of the campus. The main reason for our return to Methodism was that there was so much Christian prejudice against Unitarianism that we realized that I had little chance of obtaining a position teaching religion if that was my denomination. Among Christian churches the Methodist was my first choice, partly because of my early training in it and partly because I admired--and still do-- many good things the denomination has done. Also, we realized that intellectual growth in religion can be promoted both inside and outside Christian churches. To quote an old hymn, "Brighten the corner where you are." We also chose St. James because it was in the process of racial integration.

I was so rushed with finishing my dissertation that I did not have much time to search for vacancies. In the spring I had registered with the university's placement office, without results. Late in August I wrote to the Board of Education of the Methodist Church in Nashville, inquiring if it knew of a vacancy. Dr. Stanley H. Martin, Director of the Department of Personnel, sent me an application blank, but warned that it was "very

late in the school year to anticipate fall placement." Little did I realize that our paths would
cross again after he became president of West
Virginia Wesleyan College.

Failing to land a teaching position in my
field, I accepted an offer from Professor Parvis to
work with him in the International Greek New
Testament Project, which was moving from the
University of Chicago to Emory University in
Atlanta. I was partly prepared for the work, for I
had taken his course on textual criticism and had
worked in the Project during the preceding
Christmas vacation. Therefore in the fall Gladys
and I sold our co-op apartment and prepared to
move.

9

THE PROJECT

Atlanta is a beautiful city, especially in the spring when its ubiquitous pink blossom and white blossom dogwood trees are in bloom and in the autumn when the leaves of those trees turn red. With an elevation of about a thousand feet, it is cooler in the summer than many cities in the South. Atlanta is the leading academic center in the Southeast, with Emory University and the Atlanta University System (the latter is a cluster of black colleges). They all deserve more recognition than they have received.

I drove to Atlanta in September 1955 to begin work in the Project. Dr. Parvis took a day off from work to help me find housing. I sorely needed his guidance, for a stranger can get lost in that city with the greatest of ease. Much of the city consists of steep wooded hills and deep ravines, which prevent the use of the ancient Greek city-plan of square blocks. A street can quickly become a road with no intersections. Parvis remarked, "If you try to drive around a block, you end up a mile out in the country!" I rented an almost new townhouse in Decatur, a short drive from the Emory campus. As we learned later, the woodsy backyard was frequented by many birds, including the South's delightful mockingbirds.

After Gladys sold our apartment in Chicago, I returned there to help her pack. When the moving van had picked up our furniture, we loaded our little Studebaker to its limit and beyond, and started out before dawn. Moving is never easy, and before we got out of Chicago, we ran into one of the city's famous potholes and broke a rear spring of the car. A garage installed a new spring that forenoon, and we were soon on our way again.

Parvis had written to three libraries on Gladys' behalf, and she was offered a position in two of them. She chose the one in the catalog department of the Atlanta Public Library. Soon afterwards we transferred our church membership to the Glenn Memorial Methodist Church on the Emory campus. Within a few months a lady invited me to teach her college-age Sunday school class there. I taught a few Sundays, then she abruptly cancelled the arrangement, having discovered that, unlike her, I was not a fundamentalist. My teaching aroused the interest of a young man in the class who later came to see me repeatedly to learn more.

Metropolitan Atlanta has a wide variety of interesting sights, and Gladys and I--and her mother when she lived with us--enjoyed sightseeing immensely. A little-known museum of merit that we found was the "Fair of 1850." It contained many antebellum antiques pertaining to rural life, including education. Established by Colonel John West on his farm sixteen miles south of Atlanta, it was easily identified by its "upping

stone" at the roadside. And what is an upping
stone? This one consisted of two stones, one
higher than the other, forming steps so that a lady
could ascend them to mount, or get "up" on, a
horse.

We lived in Atlanta at a significant time in its
history. Racial tensions were high, for the
Supreme Court's famous decision in the Brown
vs. Board of Education of Topeka case was made
in 1954, only a year before we moved to Atlanta.
Some Southerners, along with some Northerners
who had moved to the South, were quite agitated
by the decision. The day I first arrived in Atlanta
I encountered the most racist statement I have
ever heard. When I asked directions in a drug-
store, the clerk, a white woman in her fifties,
thought that a Yankee like me needed to be educated, so she told me that "niggers ain't fittin' to
live." I could hardly believe my ears! What a
rough introduction to the South! In contrast,
Gladys and I later became acquainted with some
white Southerners who were very fair-minded
and strongly pro-integration.

Nevertheless, a general attitude of racial prejudice prevailed. There were still separate public
drinking fountains for blacks and whites. We met
a white professor who had just come from the
North. Because he taught at Morehouse College, a
black school in the Atlanta University System,
white neighborhoods would not rent a house or an
apartment to him. Professors of Bible in
metropolitan Atlanta met monthly to read their
research papers to each other, and they had a
similar problem. They had to hold their inte-

grated meetings either in the YWCA or in the
black colleges.

One Sunday when we were driving around in
the Georgian countryside, we happened to drive
by the Koinonia Farm, an interracial commune
about nine miles west of the town of Americus.
Koinonia, a Greek word in the New Testament,
means "fellowship" or "communion." In 1942
Clarence Jordan, a native of the area, founded the
commune of 1,400 acres in Ku Klux Klan territory. The Klan and a related bigoted group, the
White Citizens Council, harrassed the commune
continually. They forced the gasoline distributor
to cease delivering gasoline for the farm's tractors. They tried to prevent the sale of the farm's
produce; when we drove by we could see that
someone had set fire to the farm's roadside stand.
Some students at the Candler School of Theology
(Methodist) were helping the farm by selling its
eggs in Atlanta. Soon after the commune began,
some Ku Klux Klansmen came to Jordan's door
and said, "We don't let the sun set on you people
who eat with niggers." Jordan smiled, shook
hands with the nearest one, and said, "I'm mighty
proud to make the acquaintance of some folks
who have control over the sun!" [28]

To the best of my knowledge, the only integrated church in Atlanta when we lived there was
the Unitarian/Universalist Church. A year after
we moved away, we read a newspaper report that
one hundred clergymen in Atlanta had signed a
statement that their churches were open to
Negroes. What a change! The South is to be
congratulated on its racial progress since 1954.
Considering that social progress is usually slow,

the South has made great strides forward in a few decades.

In the summer following our move to Atlanta, Dr. Virginia Lacey Jones, director of the School of Library Service in Atlanta University, invited me to speak in the auditorium on the Dead Sea scrolls, which I had studied in connection with my doctoral dissertation. Dr. Jones, a black lady, was a very competent and congenial librarian who had received her doctorate from the University of Chicago's Graduate Library School. I gladly accepted her invitation, for Atlanta University was one of the cluster of academic schools for blacks, and I was eager to help the students. I recall that when I first went to see Dr. Jones, a few students had a table in the hall and were selling memberships in the NAACP, and many students were joining.

The International Greek New Testament Project, in which I worked, was so unusual that it must be explained in relation to its background. The whole New Testament was originally written in Greek. Therefore the Greek text is very important, for the precise meaning of the original words can be lost in translation. But a problem exists: What *is* the original text? What did the authors actually write? The ancient Greek manuscripts do not agree with each other in many passages, though the disagreement is often minor. The different readings are called "variants" in the text. Apart from a few fragments, even the earliest extant manuscripts were written one to three centuries after changes had already been made by scribes when they made new copies. The manuscripts cannot be checked against the original documents, for the latter are lost. The process of trying to determine the reading of the text before scribes altered it is known as "establishing the text."

As the first step in solving the problem some biblical scholars have collated the ancient manuscripts and recorded the variant readings from which textual critics select to establish the text. But some of those scholars created another problem: they recorded some variants inaccurately. British, German, and American scholars became concerned and wished to remedy the situation. Under the sponsorship of the British Committee for the Critical Greek New Testament, S. C. E. Legg produced a critical edition of the Greek text of the Gospel of Mark in 1935 and of the Gospel of Matthew in 1940. The task was too much for one man, and he, too, made errors in reporting variant readings. In 1942 Ernest C. Colwell, Allen P. Wikgren, and Merrill M. Parvis at the University of Chicago began to draw up their own plans for a new edition of the manuscript evidence for the Greek text of the New Testament. In 1948 the University of Chicago hosted a conference of 40 American and Canadian textual critics. As a result of steps taken at the annual meeting of the Society of Biblical Literature in December 1948, the Editorial Board of American textual scholars was formed; the officers of its Executive Committee were E. C. Colwell, chairman; F. C. Grant, vice-chairman; and M. M. Parvis, executive secretary. The British Committee joined with the Americans to organize the International Greek New Testament

Project in 1949. The best New Testament textual critics in America and Great Britain were members of the committees--they were too numerous to list here. In 1949 the Project began to acquire microfilms and photostats of manuscript sources; I believe it began the process of collation in 1950. The Project received grants from the Rockefeller Foundation and the Bollingen Foundation.

The plan was to collate anew the Greek manuscripts, including those recently discovered, the versions, and the patristic quotations of the whole New Testament. The results of the collations were to be published by the Clarendon Press in Oxford in the form of a critical apparatus listing the variants, verse by verse. The Project began with the Gospel of Luke. In 1950 Parvis optimistically expected that the whole New Testament would be completed by 1965. Actually, the work on Luke was not finished until recently. and the Project will not continue with the other New Testament books.29

The University of Chicago supplied the Project with a very small room in Swift Hall that served as a combined office and workroom--the most crowded workplace I have ever seen! Parvis divided his time between supervising the Project and teaching. He employed Peter Igurashi as a collator. The University of Chicago decided early in 1955 that it could no longer afford to support the Project, so that summer the Project moved to Emory University where Colwell then was vice president. Emory, too, furnished it with housing and hired Parvis as a professor with half his time allotted to the Project.

At Emory the Project occupied two rooms in
the basement of the old Physics Building. Parvis
was informal and congenial, and we soon began to
address him by his nickname, "Shorty." Harold
(Harry) Oliver and Ann Wilkin, graduate students, and I, with some part-time help from various students, collated from microfilm the Greek
text of Luke in manuscripts located in different
parts of the world, especially Europe. To insure
accuracy in our work we had a rule that each
manuscript had to be collated twice, each time by
a different collator. Whenever a collator found a
spot that was difficult to read, he or she called in
other members of the staff for consultation. A
few British scholars sent us their collations.
During two summers William H. P. Hatch of the
Episcopal Divinity School and Jacob Geerlings of
the University of Utah worked with us--both were
prominent textual critics. I recall that we disagreed with Professor Hatch's opinion that scholarly work such as we were doing should be published in Latin. He said Latin was the language of
scholars, but we said that system belonged to the
past.

We purchased a microfilm from a library in
the Georgian Republic in the Soviet Union.
Shorty commented, "Isn't it remarkable that a library in Georgia, Russia, is selling a microfilm of
a biblical manuscript to a project in Georgia,
U.S.A.?" I was surprised that libraries in the
Soviet Union (mainly Moscow and Leningrad)
had preserved ancient Christian manuscripts, even
under Stalin's dictatorship.

Each spring we had visitors in the work-
room. At swarming time the termites suddenly

emerged from the outside wall, marched in single file across the concrete floor and into the brightly lit hall, where they disappeared into an inner wall. We never did figure out the logic of the maneuver. By mutual consent, we left them alone and they left us alone.

In 1956 we compiled an "Index," a list of the variant readings that we and others had found in 99 manuscripts of the Greek text of Luke. Carol Peterson, our secretary, typed all 864 pages, using the Greek type of our Varitype typewriter. We made thirty copies, as I recall, one of which is in my library. One day Shorty held up a copy and exclaimed, "Somewhere in there is the original text of the Gospel of Luke. Find it!"

My colleagues, Ann and Harry, were native Southerners, and I admired them for having outgrown their conservative environments. They had outgrown both fundamentalism and racism, and Ann's family had disowned her on both counts.

One evening Harry and I visited the County Fair in Atlanta. At one booth a young man, trying to sell Bibles, claimed that the Bible "prophesies the coming of automobiles." I said to him, "This I have got to see. Where does the Bible do that?" He pointed to Joel 2:9a, "They shall run to and fro in the city." I observed that there is no mention of automobiles. He replied, "No, but it describes them. Isn't that what automobiles do: run to and fro in the cities?" I responded, "But people do that too. Is there any evidence that Joel is not referring to people? And where is the evidence that the verse is referring to the twentieth century?" The salesman laughed off

my questions without trying to answer them.
Actually, his quotation is a mistranslation in the
King James Version, which he was selling. The
correct translation is: "They leap upon the city,"
as in the Revised Standard Version. Also, verse 9
continues in the King James Version: "they shall
run upon the wall, they shall climb up on the _Locusts_
houses; they shall enter in at the windows like a
thief." Thus even in the salesman's Bible the rest
of the verse makes clear the fact that the verse is
describing people, not automobiles. The salesman
was guilty of the old fundamentalist trick of lifting passages out of their context. Harry delighted
in watching me take on fundamentalists, a diver-
sion I still enjoy.

While we were living in Atlanta I read two
research papers at the annual meetings of the
Society of Biblical Literature and Exegesis in
New York. At the same time I revised my doctoral dissertation for publication.

Also while in Atlanta I wrote my first journal
article, which provides tools for determining
whether an early Christian writing was written by
Jewish Christans or by gentile Christians. When
Christianity began, all adherents were Jews, but
by the middle of the first century gentiles were
joining. Some New Testament books were written by Jewish Christians and some by gentile
Christians. If we know whether an author was a
Jew or a gentile, that knowledge can help us to
understand both the book and early church history, for it enables us to detect differences in their
use of Jewish ideas. I examined ancient works
whose authors are known to be either Jews or
gentiles, and recorded the characteristic attitudes,

expressions, and ideas of each group. Then I used them to set up criteria for detecting whether an early Christian writing came from the pen of a Jewish Christian. My article, "Early Jewish-Christian Writing," was submitted to the *Journal of Biblical Literature,* but the editor, David Noel Freedman, rejected it. Next I submitted it to *The Journal of Bible and Religion,* and its editor, Professor Carl Purinton of Boston University, not only accepted it, but sent me a note praising it.

A problem in collating an ancient manuscript is that sometimes a later scribe, a so-called "corrector," made some changes in the text of a manuscript. It is a collator's duty to distinguish between the original reading and the corrector's reading in the manuscript. Usually this can be done by observing a difference in the shade of the two inks and/or by noting the difference in the way the two scribes wrote certain letters. Nevertheless, in some cases the two can not be determined from the microfilm, but examination of the actual manuscript may solve the problem. In the Project we made a list of manuscripts and the places in them where we could not solve that problem by looking at the film. Scholars know the manuscripts by their international Gregory numbers, that is, the numbers C. R. Gregory assigned to them in his system which classifies the manuscripts according to type. But libraries know them by their own number they assigned to them when they acquired them. We had a copy of Gregory's book in which he listed the library accession numbers along with his own.

Thus we knew where each manuscript was located and its accession number in the library.

In the summer of 1957 the Project sent two teams to Europe on the original Queen Elizabeth ship to examine in the manuscripts themselves the difficult spots we had found. Harry and Shorty had made a similar trip to England in 1956, and Shorty had collated there in previous years. In 1957 one team, Ann and Shorty, accompanied by Mrs. Parvis and son Paul, spent two months working in the libraries of Oxford and Cambridge Universities. As the second team, Kenneth Clark of Duke University and I examined manuscripts for seven weeks in eleven libraries in France, Spain, Italy, Switzerland, Germany, and Holland. Six more days, each way, were spent crossing the Atlantic. Kenneth had been to Europe several times, but it was all new to me. Months in advance he had made hotel reservations for us as far as Rome; at Rome we had the American Express office make reservations for us for the rest of our journey. Before the trip Kenneth had written ahead to the librarians to inform them that we would arrive on a certain date to examine specific documents in their possession. He listed the library numbers of the manuscripts and asked permission to see them. Receiving permission to examine Codex Vaticanus was a "B" genuine privilege. Few people were allowed to examine it because it is so priceless and because at that time the binding had been removed so that the leaves could be photographed. Kenneth wrote to the Librarian, who in turn had to get permission from a cardinal.

Our work proceeded on schedule, although we had various minor problems. One difficulty was that of finding the library. In most cases the library was close enough to our hotel that we walked to it instead of taking a taxi. Locating the building without a street map, or even with one, could be difficult. In Europe streets run in all sorts of directions, and they change names whenever they make a slight turn or bend. Sometimes they are so narrow that one assumes that they are not streets; for example, a narrow stairway down a steep hill can be called a street. Street names, if visible, are generally on buildings, ten feet above the sidewalk. One evening Kenneth and I were walking around in Basel, and, looking up a narrow street, I remarked, "I wonder where that crooked street goes." Without a word he turned and began walking up the street. I followed, and five minutes later we were lost!

We could easily walk past a library building without recognizing it, because often there was no library sign on the building, and the library might be only a portion of the building. After we found the building, we still had to find the library. Which exterior door should we enter? And once inside, should we turn left, go straight ahead, turn right, or go up the stairs? Signs were as scarce inside as outside the buildings. After arriving in a city in the afternoon, we made a practice of taking a walk to locate the library so that we could go directly to work the next morning without wasting time wandering around looking for it.

Another problem was that European libraries generally close for a "summer holiday" lasting from two weeks to a month; August is the favorite time. We encountered that situation at the Vatican and at the University of Basel. The Vatican solved the problem by loaning the manuscripts to a different department, which remained open, where we worked beside B. L. Ullman, the prominent American classicist and author of the Latin grammars I had studied in high school. The University of Basel solved the holiday problem for us by loaning the manuscipts to another library that was open then.

A distracting routine occurred just after opening and just before closing time in the Manuscipt Room in the *Bibliotheque Nationale* in Paris. For fifteen minutes a clerk would roll up or roll down the noisy antique shades of the very high windows. The noise and novelty tempted us to watch the performance instead of examining manuscripts.

Twice we had a little trouble with library rules. In that same Manuscript Room Kenneth absentmindedly broke the universal rule against touching the surface of ancient manuscripts with one's fingers (the oil and dirt on human hands can cause deterioration of documents). A French librarian soon asked him to obey the rule. At the Vatican both of us broke a dress code we did not know existed there. We took off our coats because Rome was having a heat wave at the time. Even though there were only two other readers in the room with us, the man at the circulation desk came over to us and asked us to put on our coats again. Why? Because it was the rule, that's why!

At first the monk in charge of the library at El Escorial in Spain was rather unfriendly and reluctant to bring out the manuscripts, even though Kenneth had written to him about them. Language was a handicap too, for he did not speak English and we did not speak Spanish. Then Kenneth displayed the letter he had received from the Vatican Library granting us permission to examine Codex Vaticanus. The monk immediately nodded and brought out the manuscripts.

The monastery libraries were usually in a medieval setting, with the library on the second or third floor in a corner of the cloister building. The most picturesque monastery was at Grottaferrata, a few miles southeast of Rome. Arriving by train, we crossed the tiny town and approached the wooden gate in the wooden wall which enclosed the cloister yard of the monastery establishment. The gate and wall were too high for us to see what was inside. We pulled the rope beside the door, ringing a small bell on the other side of the wall. We had to wait several minutes for a monk to open the gate, and no wonder, for the door of the monastery building was diagonally across the large yard--it could not have been farther from the gate. The monk led us across the cloister yard and up the stairs to the library on the third floor. From the library windows we looked out on the stone parapet wall in notched design which protected the building in medieval days. Just outside the wall was a deep moat, which long ago had ceased to be filled with water.

The most unusual feature we saw within a library was in the *Biblioteca Medici Laurenziana* in Florence. The manuscripts were vellum codices, bound with sturdy wood covers to which were fastened chains. By means of the chains the codices were locked in their places in the stacks. When the manuscripts were delivered to a reader, the chains had to come with them. That aspect was not unique. The feature that we found nowhere else was the method of transfer between stacks and reading room, which evidently were in two adjoining buildings with no door between them. A circulation clerk walked over to a hole in the wall, placed our request slips in a wooden tray, slid the tray through the wall by pushing with a pole about seven feet long, and then pulled a cord to ring a bell to alert (or wake up?) the invisible clerk in the stacks. In due time the stack clerk with his own pole pushed the tray back to the reading room and rang his own bell. Then the circulation clerk brought us the manuscripts from the tray.

Some taxi drivers in Rome were notorious for taking tourists for a ride figuratively as well as literally. One day we walked from our hotel to the American Express to arrange for the hotel reservations for the remainder of our trip. Two days later we returned to learn if the arrangments were completed. We had found it to be a long walk, so the second time we took a taxi. The driver zig-zagged around, intentionally making a longer than necessary trip. We knew, because we had made the journey on foot. When we got out of the taxi, I paid for both of us, but only two-thirds of what the meter registered, and no tip. Then I walked away, leaving him protesting loudly in Italian. Kenneth remarked, "That's the first time I ever saw anyone win an argument with a taxi driver!"

The only time that we were not either working or traveling was the weekend we spent at San
Sebastian, Spain, a resort town. No manuscripts
were there, but Kenneth said that it was such a
nice place that it was really our duty to look there
anyway! Our hotel, the Maria Christina, had the
largest and most elegant rooms we had on the
trip, with marble everywhere and private baths.
Gladys and I drove past it in 1985, and I was sad-
dened to see that the hotel, once so magnificent,
was so deteriorated 28 years later. The old Felix
Hotel in Paris was a sharp contrast to the Maria
Christina. Selected because of its proximity to the
Bibliotheque Nationale, it was our cheapest hotel
($2 per day with continental breakfast). Its bath
was a common tub on the landing between the
second and third floors. Its plumbing was quite
unreliable. When Kenneth, in the room above
mine, drained his lavatory, the water gurgled up
into my lavatory.

Some experiences with manuscripts were
thrilling to us, though they might not excite laymen. At the Vatican we handled and examined
Codex Vaticanus, labeled Codex B in Gregory's
system. This famous manuscript, once stolen by
Napoleon, is still the earliest (mid-fourth century)
and best extant manuscript source of much of the
New Testament. In Basel we examined another
famous manuscript, Gregory 1. Erasmus used it
as the primary basis of his printed Greek text of
the New Testament, the text which later became
the basis of the so-called *Textus Receptus,*
"Received Text," from which the King James
Version was essentially translated. In the margin
of Gregory 1 we saw the marks Erasmus made

when he collated the codex, and in the text the marks the printer made to denote the end of each printed page.   At the Bodmer Library near Cologny, Switzerland, we were shown a leaf of the newly discovered Papyrus Bodmer II; except for small fragments, it is one of the two earliest extant manuscripts of the Gospel of John (ca. A.D. 200).

We also translated an early Christian talisman. Before and during the first six centuries of the Christian era the Egyptians and others wrote magic formulae on tiny scrolls and hung them around their necks to ward off evil spirits. These tiny scrolls constituted one form of talisman, a good luck charm. When Christianity spread to Egypt, many Egyptian Christians adapted the practice to their new faith by writing biblical verses on tiny scrolls and wearing them as talismans. In the *Biblioteca Medici Laurenziana* in Florence we collated one, T4 (T stands for Talisman), a fifth- or sixth- century papyrus about two inches high and about eight inches wide. Written across the long way were John 1:1; Matt. 1:1; Mark 1:2; Luke1:1; half of Psalm 90:1 (in the Greek Septuagint version, which is 91:1 in the Hebrew and English texts); and the Doxology. The talisman was in fragmentary condition and mounted between glass plates.

Not all of our interesting experiences pertained to manuscripts. St. Peter's Cathedral impressed me as a magnificent museum, not a church. We stayed at the Columbus Hotel nearby; it was originally a Franciscan abbey and was in the process of being converted into a hotel and restaurant.   Going from the sublime to the ridiculous, I recall the Hotel Schottenhamel in Munich. In its restaurant we had a bit of an argument with a waiter. The same entree was listed twice in the menu, as a single order for one person and as a double order for two. Strangely, the cost of two single orders was less than the double order, so we each ordered a single. The waiter, however, insisted on the double order. After five minutes of argument in broken German and broken English, we wore down the waiter's resistance and won the battle without starting World War III. Hotel Schottenhamel had the distinction of being the only hotel I have ever known with its name printed on each section of the rolls of toilet tissues. In those days toilet tissue in Europe was harsher than in America; Kenneth called it "sandpaper."

When we finished our work in Geneva, Kenneth went on to Austria (to the Salzburg Music Festival) and to Wolfenbüttel, West Germany (to continue our work), while I went to the University of Utrecht to examine manuscripts. After depositing our collations and notes with Shorty in Oxford, I sailed home on the Queen Mary; its worn joints rattled so much that I could hardly sleep at night. The trip was a great experience and prepared me for the numerous photographic expeditions to Europe that Gladys and I have made in recent years.

When I had left for Europe, Gladys had driven to Oregon for the summer, accompanied by her mother and her Aunt Josie Windedahl Kellogg. In August, leaving her mother at home in Salem, Gladys took her aunt home to Michigan and then drove on to Mansfield, Ohio. There she met me when I got off the train from New York. It was August 22, her birthday, and we had a grand celebration, after having been apart for more than two months--it seemed like two years!

In the spring of the year I had looked for a teaching position, but found none. I preferred teaching to collating manuscripts, and I rightly feared that the Project might run out of funds. When I had given up hope, I received a telephone call from Corwin Roach, dean at Bexley Hall, inviting me to come for an interview for a temporary position. I had been recommended to him by Amos Wilder at Harvard Divinity School, formerly my professor when he was chairman of the New Testament Department at Chicago. He was the brother of the playwright, Thornton Wilder. I flew to Mansfield, and a student at Kenyon College drove me to Gambier for the interview. I got the job.

After two years at Emory, the Project found itself in debt, so its operations and staff were reduced to a bare minimum. Only Shorty and Ann remained. Dr. Colwell became president of the new Methodist seminary at Claremont, the Southern California School of Theology, and in 1965 the Project was moved there. After he retired, the Project's work was scattered; I learned that Kenneth Clark at Duke and Eldon Jay Epp at Case-Western Reserve Universities continued the work. At last the work is now completed, and the results have recently been published by Clarendon Press in Oxford, as it had agreed some thirty-five years earlier.[30] In addition to the versions and patristic quotations, the Project collated a total of

238 manuscripts containing all or part of the Greek text of the Gospel of Luke.

10

BEXLEY HALL

Bexley Hall was a seminary of the Protestant Episcopal Church, located at one end of the campus of Kenyon College in Gambier, Ohio. Construction of the stone building, in modified English Gothic style, began in 1839. The exterior is beautiful, today ivy-clad. The seminary has since moved to Rochester, New York, to join with Colgate and Crozer seminaries. The town of Gambier consisted of a few houses, the college, seminary, Church of the Holy Spirit, post office, general store with gas pumps outside, and the nationally famous restaurant, the Village Inn. A small Methodist church was on the border.

Oscar J. F. Seitz, professor of New Testament at Bexley Hall, was granted a sabbatical leave for the academic year 1957-58, which he and his wife Ruth spent in research at Oxford University. I was fortunate to have the opportunity to fill the vacancy. My rank was only Visiting Instructor, but even a temporary position enabled me to get my start in teaching. Gladys and I enjoyed living in the Seitz's comfortable house, watching the wood burn in the Franklin heater in the winter, and sitting on the screened front porch in the summer. Their home contained many early American antiques. A variety of birds came in the winter to dine on the feeder shelves the Seitz had attached to the sills of the kitchen windows. We watched cardinals and titmice eat there, and they peered through the kitchen window and watched us eat. Commuting to work was easy; Bexley Hall was only a block away.

The seminary's library, Colburn Library, was a wing attached at right angles at the rear of Bexley Hall, constructed in the old English manner. The book shelves continued up the high walls to the ceiling, and the upper shelves were reached either by the tall ladder on rollers or by ascending the stairs to the narrow balcony. Mrs. Agnes Roach, the librarian, took a leave of absence, and Gladys was asked to be the acting librarian for the academic year. Gladys cataloged 670 new titles and operated the library alone, except that a student handled the circulation desk in the evenings.

Corwin Roach was a congenial dean to work with, and he made a special effort to help me learn the ways of an Episcopal seminary. My main problem was the chapel. As a member of the small faculty I took my turn every fifth Thursday at conducting the weekly evening prayer in the chapel. The relatively informal services in Methodist and Unitarian churches had left me quite unprepared to lead the students in the frequent standing up and sitting down and in chanting strange ritual I had never heard, with its rhythm I had to learn. Dean Roach gave me a copy of *The Book of Common Prayer* to use, and I wrote the order of service inside the front cover to guide me. Students and faculty alike wore black robes during chapel, another feature to which I was unaccustomed. One aspect, however, was easier than in Methodist and Unitarian services, namely, prayer. Instead of having to think up what to say next, I merely had to read aloud a few prayers from *The Book of Common Prayer*.

The student body was small, comprised of thirty young men. The courses I taught were the Gospel of John, introduction to the New Testament, and elementary New Testament (that is, Hellenistic) Greek. During the second semester I taught archaeology to a group of five students; the class met in our home Wednesday evenings. At first all the students wondered, "What's that Methodist doing on the faculty? We want to learn Episcopalianism, not Methodism." Because they did not trust my biblical interpretation, I assigned each one a separate small project to investigate in the New Testament. With that system they did not have to believe my teaching; they were tested in examinations on how much information they had found. When they found the evidence themselves, they paid attention to it. Because the Episcopal Church has its roots in the Church of England, I selected for the course on the Gospel of John a textbook written by a British professor, C. K. Barrett. The students soon accepted me and we became good friends. At the end of the school year some students gave me a new copy of *The Book of Common Prayer* and inscribed it with a tribute to me in appreciation.

The students published a weekly newsletter, "The Megiddo Plain Dealer," edited by Bruce

Whitehead. A November issue reported that in his recent sermon in chapel Dr. Teeple said that churches have been too slow to adjust their doctrine to modern knowledge, and that "theologically it is time to halt the 'hold that line' policy and go to 'forward pass.'" I still say "Amen" to that!

One Sunday we attended the service in the Methodist church at Gambier, but the sermon was so mediocre that Gladys and I never returned. Soon afterwards we joined the Gay Street Methodist Church in Mount Vernon, five miles distant. The situation in that church was much more to our liking. With justifiable pride the congregation told us that their church had once been the home church of Dr. Ralph W. Sockman, the famous liberal Methodist minister in New York whose sermons I had heard live on our radio in Oregon thirty years earlier. Through the month of March 1959 I gave the Wednesday-evening Lenten series lectures in that church; the subject was the Gospel of Mark. Afterwards Reverend John Taylor, the minister, thanked me "for the splendid way in which you conducted the study of Mark."

My favorite Bexley story is that of an incident reported to me by a student. When the student's test paper was returned to him after an examination, he found an illegible comment by the professor written in the margin. Going to the professor's office, the student pointed to the comment and asked, "What does this say?" The professor replied, "It says, 'I can't read your writing.'" Both men were poor penmen, and I guess they deserved each other.

Some students were obsessed with the idea that theology is the most important aspect of religion, but I emphasized the idea that ethics is the most important. This, of course, is not a new issue in religion. Once a student and I were standing in the hall, debating this issue, and I pointed to the Golden Rule in the Sermon on the Mount, the fact that one of the Two Commandments in Mark 12 is "love your neighbor as yourself," and especially the pericope, or unit, in Mark 10:17-22. In this last passage a man asks Jesus what he must do to "inherit eternal life." In his reply Jesus does not even mention theological doctrines or belief in himself. Instead, he lists six of the Ten Commandments and adds the injunction to "sell what you have and give to the poor." My student objected, "But that's just Judaism!" I replied ironically, "Well, isn't that just too bad!"He, like others, pointed to the Gospel of John, in which Jesus is presented as demanding belief in himself as the Son of the Father. The student was unaware that this gospel presents Jesus in terms of Hellenistic mysticism, a type of thought foreign to Jesus and his environment.

The brightest of my Bexley Hall students was F. Allyn Walker. A musical genius, he had been the organist and choir director at All Saints Episcopal Church in Cincinnati for ten years, and he had taught music theory at Cincinnati Conservatory. He excelled at composing organ music. His wife Patricia was also musically talented and sang contralto; sometimes they gave concerts together. Eager to learn more than I was able to provide in my courses, Allyn borrowed books from my library and became especially interested in my specialty, textual criticism. One of the books he borrowed contained the Greek text of the Gospel of John in Papyrus Bodmer II as transliterated by Professor Victor Martin of the University of Geneva. (Often ancient manuscripts are hard to read, with indistinct letters and no spaces between words. Before they are officially translated, someone transliterates the text by printing it clearly to facilitate study and translation.) This book contains photographs of three pages of the manuscript. Allyn compared the photographs with Martin's transliteration of them and showed me some errors that Martin had made. Then, applying techniques I had learned in the Project, together we carefully examined the photographs. We wrote an article recording the errors we found in the transliteration of the three pages, and concluded by calling for publication of facsimiles (photographs) of the whole manuscript as soon as possible. Scholars were already beginning to cite it, and they should have the actual text to work with, not an erroneous reproduction of it. Our article was published in the *Journal of Biblical Literature* in 1959. Within a few years Kenneth Clark and others, following our lead, exerted their influence on the Bodmer Library, which published facsimiles of the whole manuscript in 1962.

Gladys and I visited the Walkers in the summer of 1959 in Columbus, Ohio, and the next summer they visited us. I remember that when we were in their home, Allyn spent half an hour on the telephone talking to a member of his church, dissuading her from committing suicide. I admired his patience. When the Walkers visited us, Allyn and I discovered a new technique for detecting the penmanship of two different scribes in a manuscript. We discovered it while we were solving a problem in textual criticism.

The British Museum found, through the use of ultra-violet light, that in Codex Sinaiticus the Gospel of John ended with 21:24, and that someone added verse 25 afterward. Our problem was to determine whether verse 25 was added by the same scribe who wrote the manuscript or was added by one of the correctors of the codex. Most textual critics have opted for the original scribe, but Constantin Tischendorf, the great New Testament scholar of the nineteenth century, concluded that verse 25 was added by a corrector. The basis of judging the matter is comparison of the penmanship. Allyn and I photographed British Museum plates of the ending of John in Sinaiticus to make slides; then we projected the slides on to a large screen; next we held sheets of paper on the screen and traced various letters; finally we held tracings of those letters over the letters in another place on the screen. The value of this method is that the large magnification enables one to detect more fully differences in the way two different scribes wrote the letters. We concluded that Tischendorf was right. The significance of the conclusion is that it increases the probability that 21:25 was added to John later, a conclusion suggested also by that verse's variation in style, syntax, and thought from the rest of the gospel, which the French scholar L. Vaganay observed. Thus John grew in three stages: the original, chapters 1-20; second stage, 21:1-24 was added; third stage, 21:25 was added.

Thereafter the fate of the Walkers was tragic. Patricia, a lovely woman, died of cancer a few year later. In the 1970s we received a telephone call from Allyn's second wife, Barbara, in Webster Groves, Missouri, where he was then pastor. She reported that Allyn's personality had changed drastically, and she wondered if I could help. A year later she told us that the cause of his abnormality had proved to be a brain tumor. Allyn had had tremendous potential, and if he had remained healthy, he surely would have made important creative contributions to the world.

In the spring of our year at Bexley Hall an unhappy event occurred: a student rebellion. Apparently there were several causes. First, at that time Christian existentialism was a fad prevalent in seminaries and popular with theologians. It is a pessimistic metaphysical theology that is anti-science and anti-reason in outlook. Its roots are in Kierkegaard's obsession with man's emotional and spiritual "existence," his contention that all truth is subjective, and his claim that man's real condition is his anxiety about life and death. Existentialism developed and became widespread in Europe and America after 1918. Karl Barth was an early exponent. The underlying cause of it was a pessimistic psychology, disillusion with man and the world, based on abnormal conditions. In Kierkegaard's case, it was his own melancholy youth. In society it was disillusion resulting from the Great Depression, two world wars, Nazism, and communism that induced some theologians to espouse it. Dean Roach kept his feet on the ground and did not fall for the fad, but some Bexley students thought he was thereby old-fashioned and that he should adopt the "new" theology.

The second cause of the rebellion was the isolation of the school. The student bodies of both Kenyon College and Bexley Hall were all male, and historically both groups became restless in the spring, for tiny Gambier was virtually devoid of young women. Sexually segregated schools do not provide a normal environment, especially when all the other sex are miles away. Two-thirds of the Bexley students were single. Several professors told me that they believed that sexual frustration intensified the students' theological frustration. A third factor, according to students' complaints, was that the dean was not flexible enough in dealing with them. I listened to the students and discussed the matter with Dean Roach. I liked both him and the students, but I agreed with him. He was a good scholar and a good teacher, but some students failed to recognize those attributes. Only a few started the trouble, but they propagandized others and took their case to the local bishop and to the new president of Kenyon College. As a Methodist in an Episcopalian school, I was an outsider and had to be neutral. But I was disheartened to see what was happening to a man with such a distinguished career. Dean Roach had received his B.D. degree *summa cum laude* from Yale Divinity School and his Ph.D. from Yale Graduate School. He was the author of three books and was largely responsible for the development of Bexley Hall. The Philadelphia Divinity School in 1957 awarded him the honorary degree of Doctor of Sacred

Theology "in recognition of his notable service to the church and nation in training men for spiritual leadership." Bexley gave him a year's sabbatical leave, but did not renew his contract. The affair advanced his career, however, for he became director of the North Dakota School of Religion at North Dakota State University, continuing there until his retirement. The affair illustrates the danger of people being carried away by fads, theological or otherwise.

In the spring I registered with the Methodist Placement Bureau in Nashville, the American College Bureau in Chicago, and the University of Chicago's Office of Career Placement. The Methodist agency reported that there were more than four applicants for every vacancy they had in teaching religion. The commercial agency had one vacancy listed which appeared to be a possibility, so I asked it to forward my credentials to the school, West Virginia Wesleyan College in Buckhannon, a Methodist college as the word "Wesleyan" indicates, with about 1200 students.

Gladys and I accepted an invitation from Martha and Harry Oliver to visit them during spring vacation that year. After graduating from Emory, Harry had obtained a teaching position at Southeastern Baptist Theological Seminary in Wake Forest, North Carolina. (He later advanced to Boston University School of Theology.) We had never been in West Virginia, so Gladys and I drove over to Buckhannon to see Wesleyan's campus on our way to the Olivers. We found that, except for its hilly setting, the campus re-

minded us of my Methodist undergraduate alma
mater, Willamette University. (Incidentally, Dr.
Doney, president of Willamette during my first
two years there, was formerly president of W.
Va. Wesleyan.) Because it was a Saturday, the
campus was almost deserted. I wandered into the
old administration building and found an open
door. I entered, and hard at work at his desk--as
usual, I learned later--was the dean, Dr. Arthur
Schoolcraft.

Dean Schoolcraft and I had a long, cordial
visit. He pulled my application out of a file of
thirty he had received and asked questions about
myself. Finally, he told me of a "dream" that he
and the local district superintendent of the
Methodist Church had had for several years.
Now that the college had a new president, Dr.
Stanley Martin, he hoped that the college might finance the project.

"We have many men with Local Preacher's
Licenses, serving from one to six tiny churches in
these mountains. None of them have attended
college or seminary, and many of them have not
even graduated from high school."

"My God!," I exclaimed.

"Our dream," he said, "is to raise the educational level of these fellows, hoping that some
will attend our college and go on to seminary.
The plan is that the district superintendent would
organize them into a weekly class on interpreting
the Bible. Our college would furnish a professor
to drive out fifty miles to teach the course.
Would you be interested in doing that?"

"I might have some trouble communicating
with them, because there is bound to be a big gap

between what I have learned at the University of Chicago and elsewhere and what they believe. Nevertheless, I am willing to try and will do the best I can."

"I'll talk to President Martin about it. There are these other applicants to consider too, but I'll let you know the results as soon as I can."

We shook hands, and Gladys and I drove on to Wake Forest to spend a delightful Easter with the Olivers. Around the middle of April I received a telephone call inviting Gladys and me to come to stay on Wesleyan's campus for an interview. While we were there Professor (of history) George Glauner and wife Marcia Mae drove us around, and so did Professor (of religious education) Sidney Davis, showing us the campus and town. We were favorably impressed, especially with the friendliness of everyone. I also appreciated the fact that both the president and dean were graduates of a liberal school, Boston University School of Theology. Later President Martin mailed a contract to me, and I eagerly signed. My starting salary for the nine-month academic year was $5,300 and my rank was Associate Professor.

11

WEST VIRGINIA WESLEYAN COLLEGE

Not without good reason is West Virginia called the "Mountain State." A positive result of the mountains is that the scenery is absolutely gorgeous when the leaves turn color in the autumn. The large variety of maples and other trees insures a wide range of bright colors. West Virginia deserves more tourist trade in the fall than it has received.

The mountains have two negative effects, however. The more serious is economic. Tillable land is so scarce that agriculture is virtually impossible in most of the state. West Virginia was once endowed with a huge quantity of coal, but most of the coal that was profitable to mine has gone, with the profits going largely to out-of-state corporations. Consequently West Virginia is now an impoverished state. It has many fine citizens, but most lack wealth. The state does produce some excellent glassware, which deserves more recognition.

The second negative effect of the mountains is on the roads. A straight road is expensive to build in mountains, and in the 1950s a straight road there was harder to find than a good man anywhere. Before I accepted the position at

Wesleyan, I looked at a map and saw that Pittsburgh and Washington, D.C. were not far from Buckhannon, as the crow flies. I thought I could use the libraries in those cities to continue my research on Christian origins. I did not realize how long it would take to travel by automobile or by train. By now some better highways have been built. The nature of the roads at that time is illustrated by the drive from Buckhannon to the mountain towns where I taught the extension course that I had promised Dean Schoolcraft I would be willing to teach. In the fifty-mile drive, there was only one stretch of straight road, about a quarter of a mile long. Dean Schoolcraft rode with me when I drove to the first session of the course. At one point a hairpin turn was so extreme that the road almost doubled back into itself. Pointing with his thumb at the bank between us and the section of the road we had just driven over, he laughingly remarked, "I'll bet it isn't more than three feet through there!"

During my job interview we learned that a retired Methodist District Superintendent, Thomas Zumbrunnen, and his wife were building a small house a block and half from the campus, and that it might be possible to rent it for a year while he temporarily returned to a pastorate. In the summer we made the rental agreement and moved in before the interior was finished.

When we were moving a carload of our belongings to Buckhannon, I stopped one night at a cottage in the West Virginia mountains to inquire about the road. Before the woman who came to the door could give me directions, her son, about four years old, said to his mother, "He looks like Jesus." Both the mother and I were embarrassed, and I quickly said, "No, I don't think so." I noticed a stylized portrait of Jesus on the wall, and guessed that the child's parents may have emphasized the picture as they were beginning to give him religious training. Another factor could have been the isolated location of the home; the child probably saw few strangers, and when one suddenly appeared on a stormy night, the boy might think that he "looks like Jesus."

After I signed my job contract, Dean Schoolcraft and I decided what courses I should teach: three sections of "New Testament History" (a three-hour course for freshmen), three hours of "Church History," and three hours of "Basic Christian Faith." Although I knew early church history very well, my knowledge of subsequent Christian history was inadequate. Therefore I studied the subject all summer and worked up lesson plans for the course. But on registration day in September very few students signed up for "Church History," so the dean dropped it from the schedule. He asked me to teach "World Religions" instead, although I had not taken a single course in the subject! Consequently I stumbled along throughout the first semester, trying to keep ahead of the students in reading the textbook, which is no way to teach. To provide some variety and some acquaintance with source material, I read aloud in class excerpts from English translations of the ancient literature of the religions. Some days I did not have time to read the source material before class. On one of those days I encountered some very sexy stuff in the Hindu writings. I had to stop in the middle of a sentence, and the students laughed, for they guessed what my problem was. It was the most embarrassing moment of my teaching career, but the students--bless their hearts--kindly overlooked it.

The first year I got off to a bad start with the three large sections of the New Testament course for freshmen. I was too lenient in maintaining order. Some students persisted in talking to each other in class in spite of my frequent calls for quiet, for they did not take me seriously. In the fourth week I expelled two students for talking in one section, to everyone's surprise. The next day the two begged to be readmitted and promised to behave. I let them in again, the word quickly spread, and thereafter all went well in all three sections. In the following years I had no problem because I insisted on order beginning the very first day.

The chairman of the Bible Department was Professor Ralph Brown, who had taught at Wesleyan for 36 years. To my astonishment, he was still using *New Testament History,* by Harris F. Rall, published in 1904, as the textbook in the freshmen New Testament course. The book was good in its day, but biblical scholars had learned a lot in the following 54 years. In my first year at Wesleyan, as a member of the Bible Department, I had to use the same textbook. I supplemented it with much factual information, but I did not enjoy using a textbook that I frequently had to correct. The next year the administration got me out of my predicament by creating a new department, the Religion Department, and appointing me chairman. Then I was able to choose a recent textbook. To introduce the course I worked up a syllabus and distributed it to the students to provide additional historical background for New Testament study. My version of the course, which included the showing of slides, was very popular. In fairness to Dr. Brown, I must give him credit for being liberal in theology. I especially appreciated his apt comment on fundamentalism: "They who say they believe the Bible 'from civver to civver' are not aware of all that is between the civvers." With a twinkle in his eye, he deliberately mispronounced "cover" as "civver."

My extension class met in the Methodist church in the town of Gassaway during the first semester, and in the Methodist church in Sutton the second. Teaching modern biblical scholarship to mountaineers--some middle-aged, some young--with Methodist Local Preacher's Licenses was an unusual and very rewarding experience. As Dean Schoolcraft had told me, none of these students had had much education, and I rightly assumed that virtually all were fundamentalists. Although the Methodist publications were rather conservative, they were not fundamentalist. But some of the tiny churches did not use Methodist materials in their Sunday school. Fundamentalists traveled around in the mountains, urging Methodist churches not to use the materials published by their own denomination, but to use David C. Cook Sunday school materials instead. These people even stood on street corners in Buckhannon, preaching and teaching, urging passersby to use "a black-backed Bible" (King James Version), not a "red-backed Bible" (Revised Standard Version).

In some mountain churches not only was education regarded with disdain, but also the practice of the preacher was not to prepare his sermons. Instead, he stepped up to the pulpit, opened the Bible, read aloud whatever passage his eyes landed on, and then preached from that text, relying on the Holy Spirit to tell him what to say.

To communicate effectively with the extension class, I relied mainly on two principles:

1. *Keep both the material and methods as simple as possible* . This was necessary because the students had had too little education to absorb much knowledge at a time. At each class session I began by writing a question on a blackboard, and the students copied it on paper. Then I gave the answer orally, and continued by writing on the blackboard a summary of the answer, which the students copied. Then on to the next question and answer. We discussed the questions as we came to them, and before the end of the class session I handed out a sheet summarizing and supplementing the lesson. This low level of pedagogy would never do in a college setting, but in an isolated mountain setting it worked out very well.

2. *In the first semester, present the background of the Bible and the historical methods of studying the book.* This approach was desirable because it was relatively non-controversial and because it helped the students to understand the Bible when they studied it later. Description of the individual books of the Bible was presented in the second semester.

The topic of the first session was, "In what languages was the Bible originally written?" That topic was more controversial than I had expected,

for a few students thought that the Bible was
originally written in God's own language, namely,
King James English! Also, I made the mistake of
using the earlier Creation story (Genesis 2:4b-25)
to illustrate the value of knowing the original languages, Hebrew and Greek. I pointed out that the
word "Adam" in the King James Version is a
transliteration of the Hebrew word *adom*, which
means "mankind," whereas *ish* is the Hebrew
term that denotes an individual "man." Two of
the 25 students never came back. Nevertheless,
by the end of the semester, there were 30 in the
class.

The topic of the second session was, "What
are the sources of the English translations of the
New Testament?" For this I showed slides I had
made as a result of my experience in the Project
in Atlanta. The slides showed examples of the
types of Greek New Testament manuscripts and of
the ways in which scribes changed the text when
they transmitted it through the centuries. The
slides demonstrated that the King James Version is
not translated from the original text because its
translators had access only to late manuscripts
containing altered texts. At the close of the first
session I had not been sure whether the course
would be a success or not, but the manuscript
slides in the second session turned the tide in the
right direction. After viewing the slides, a student, Mack Boggs, came to me after class and
said, "I'm just beginning to realize how little I
know about this!" I replied, "Cheer up, you have
taken the first step essential for learning. You are
on your way!"

The lack of educational background of some students was manifest the first time I gave an examination. Two men copied from each other during the exam and even discussed the questions. I put a stop to it good-naturedly, and everyone laughed. Those two mountaineers had no intention of cheating; they simply were unfamiliar with examinations.

Dr. W. Reese Burns, the District Superintendent of the Methodist Central District in West Virginia, encouraged the students to take the course by attending regularly himself during the first semester. He did not come the second semester because he knew the students were enthusiastic and would attend without any pressure from him. Relations among us all were very cordial, and at the end of the course the students gave me an expensive briefcase as a token of appreciation. I was almost embarrassed to accept it, for I knew that with their tiny incomes they could hardly afford it. The initial chasm between mountaineers with little education and very conservative in religion, on one side, and a teacher liberal in religion, with a Ph.D. in Bible, on the other side, was bridged. Most important, several of them decided to go on to college and seminary; one of them was Mack Boggs.

About a month after I began teaching at Wesleyan, two fundamentalist students decided that my "Basic Christian Faith" course was not conservative enough in doctrine, so they went to Dean Schoolcraft and asked that I be dismissed from the faculty. His response was to loan them his copy of Albert Schweitzer's book, *The Quest for the Historical Jesus,* and to ask them to read it, which they did. The dean never told me what had happened behind my back, but after the two young men were intellectually awakened by him, they told me themselves and apologized. We became very good friends, and they became staunch advocates of the historical approach to the Bible.

During the Christmas vacation of our first year at Wesleyan, the industrious Dean Schoolcraft worked in his office, in spite of the fact that the administration building was unheated during the holidays. He caught a cold, which quickly developed into pneumonia. Taken to the hospital, he soon had a stroke and died at the age of 61. He had received his A.B. degree *summa cum laude* from Marietta College, and an S.T.B. *summa cum laude* and a Ph.D. from Boston University. Orlo Strunk, Jr., professor of psychology, became the new dean.

Buckhannon had two Methodist churches, First and Central. At First Methodist Church the minister, the Reverend Samuel Harford, and the laymen were better educated and more liberal in theology than at Central. Gladys and I joined First.

Gladys worked part-time in the college library. She was also active in various women's organizations in Buckhannon: the College Club, the Buckhannon Woman's Club, and the local branch of the American Association of University Women. She also joined the Woman's Society of Christian Service at church, and in March 1960 she taught a series of lessons on the portrait of Jesus in the Gospel of Luke.

At the end of our first academic year we bought a two-story frame house at 169 Fayette

Street, about five blocks from the campus. The
house was in worse condition than we realized
when we bought it, but after we repaired it, we
had a comfortable home. Gladys loved the fireplace.

For my second and third years at Wesleyan
I chose as the textbook for the introductory New
Testament course *Understanding the New
Testament,* by Howard Kee and Franklin Young.
At the first class session I wrote on the blackboard
the title and the names of the authors so that the
students would know what to ask for at the book-
store. Carelessly I misspelled Professor Kee's
name as "Key," and a student who had already
purchased his copy laughed and corrected me.
What a way for a professor to begin the school
year!

The president of Wesleyan, Dr. Stanley
Martin, and his energetic wife, Glenadene,
worked unstintingly to develop the college. He,
Schoolcraft, and Strunk were administrators who
fostered research by the faculty. Under Strunk's
initiative the college launched a new annual journal, *Wesleyan Studies in Religion,* to encourage
faculty scholarship.

In the summer of 1960 the faculty committee granted me $150 from the small Wesleyan re-
search fund to photograph Greek New Testament
manuscripts and copy old pictures. The purpose
was to complete four slide lectures I had begun. I
took my own copying equipment along and photographed in the Special Collections Department
(rare books) of the library of the University of
Chicago. I also checked out books from departmental libraries at the university and pho-

tographed from them in my hotel room. In the following academic year I showed the slides in my sections of the "New Testament History" course, and donated a set of each slide lecture to the college. I showed the slides on Mithraism to the Upshur County Historical Society and to the Wesleyan faculty. Professor George Keester of the Art Department and I teamed up to present a joint program on Christian art; I presented my slide lecture on the early Christian frescoes in the catacombs at Rome, and he followed it with his slide lecture on European cathedrals.

The students at Wesleyan were admirable, and Gladys and I enjoyed our association with them. I insisted that they study hard, and I worked hard myself to give them all the education I could. In giving examinations and grades, I made a special effort to be fair. At the beginning of each course I announced the basis of grading, and I emphasized that all students would be graded on the amount of their knowledge of the facts, and not on whether they agreed with my beliefs or with traditional doctrines. "What you believe is your own business," I said.

My most outstanding student was Arnold Nelson from Long Island, New York. He was older than the average student because he had served in the Army. He took all his undergraduate courses in three years and graduated *cum laude*. We had much in common, for he, too, had started to be a Methodist minister and had abandoned the plan when he learned how far behind churches were in their understanding of the Bible and Christian origins. After graduation he earned a master's degree at Long Island University and a

Ph.D. at Texas Christian University--both degrees were in psychology. Today he is a practicing psychologist in Winston-Salem and a member of the board of directors of the Religion and Ethics Institute (see chapter below).

One student was very disappointing, I must admit. She had read some of Ayn Rand's books and fully accepted her philosophy of selfishness. The student was strongly opposed to social action, and said that she agreed with William F. Buckley that compassion and helping people does not belong in religion. Ironically, she was majoring in religious education and was a leader in the campus Methodist Youth Movement. She was in my "Christianity and the Social Order" course, and we spent a whole class period debating the question, Should the church be concerned with social welfare? Everyone else answered "Yes" to the question. One student, Bob Braden, reported that in his small pastorate in the mountains he had seen children brought to church without shoes because their parents could not afford them. He asked, "Shouldn't the church be concerned about such conditions?" We failed to convince the young lady, but I hope that she changed her views later.

Chaperoning dances was a very pleasant way to get to know the students informally. The newly organized local chapter of the Phi Sigma Epsilon fraternity asked me to be one of its advisors during our last year at Wesleyan. I attended the initiation of new members and laughed and laughed at the pranks. And I had thought that my boyhood buddy Vernon had already thought of all the tricks that could be played on people!

A small college in an isolated small town is quite dependent on the town and the town on it. In Buckhannon relations between the two were cordial with no "town vs. gown" atmosphere. During the first winter we were in Buckhannon the Sigma Eta Epsilon fraternity sponsored a basketball game for the benefit of the American Red Cross. The two teams were the White Collar Whizzes (local businessmen) and Faculty Flashes (Wesleyan faculty). For some inexplicable reason I, who had never learned to play basketball, was chosen as one of the eleven members of the Flashes. Someone at school assigned to us nicknames such as "Rowdy" Ross, "Wild" Willis, and "Tipsy" Teeple. After the first practice session the faculty coach wisely demoted me to the rank of one of the clowns for the occasion. One of the antics of the clowns at the game was to throw extra basketballs onto the court to further confuse the already confused players. Once during the game, while I was standing on the sideline, I grabbed the player's basketball and tossed it at a basket. To everyone's surprise--especially mine-- the ball went through the hoop. The next day the students in my "Christianity and the Social Order" class presented me with a "sports letter" award, a W which they had cut out of paper and a citation which stated " . . . may you continue to proceed in your further pursuits in the field of eschatology, avoiding any other attempts on the basketball court."

We formed some close friendships with some of the faculty and students. Among them were Dr. George Glauner, professor of history, and his wife Marcia Mae; he had a delightful sense of humor. He used to say, "The surprising thing about attending alumni reunions is to see how much older everyone else looks."

Our closest friends on the faculty were Dr. Kenneth and Ann Plummer. At the same time that I was made chairman of the Religion Department, the administration employed him as an associate professor in that department. Ken was a graduate of Garrett Biblical Institute and of the Divinity School of the University of Chicago. He had held Methodist pastorates in Illinois, Iowa, Wisconsin, and West Virginia. He was popular as a preacher and a teacher, a marvelous storyteller, and intellectually progressive. He was a grand colleague.

Ken told me that a student of his, who was pastor of a small church in the mountains of West Virginia, had to be away one Sunday, so he asked Ken if he would preach in his place that day. Ken gladly consented. The student told him that all he would have to do would be to preach the sermon, for a lay leader would conduct the service. So Ken drove over many miles of winding roads to the church, where about twenty members were waiting in the pews. The lay leader started things off by asking in a mountaineer twang, "Well, folks, what number would you like to sing this morning?" Some brave soul called out, "Number 102." The leader realized that they were in trouble, because number 102 was not one of the ten old standby hymns that were in the little congregation's repertoire. He looked at the organist sitting at the old footpump organ and asked, "Lem, can you play that one?" Lem's pride was hurt, and raising his chin, said stoutly. "If the folks can sing

it, I can play it." So they began, but after a few
bars, it was obvious that Lem could not play it.
The lay leader handled the situation quite tactfully. Calling out above the noise, he said,
"Whoa, whoa, folks, hold it. Lem, I don't think
the folks can sing that one!"

I wish that the story of the Plummers had a
happy ending, but it doesn't. Ann had myasthenia
gravis, and her life was one of frequent trips to
Pittsburgh for tests and treatment. Some days she
was confined to bed. Life would surely have been
unbearable for her if it had not been for a new
Japanese drug which doctors gave her along with
other pills. Ann had a sense of humor too, and
each week Ken alleviated her stress by posting
new jokes and cartoons on a bulletin board in the
kitchen.

After Gladys and I left Wesleyan, Ken was
promoted to my position of departmental chairman. That summer the Plummers visited us in
Chicago. We spent an evening together on
Promontory Point, a park jutting out into Lake
Michigan at the end of 55th Street. Sitting on the
lawn, in a cool breeze, Ken and I told jokes until
11 P.M., but I could not keep up with him.
Amazed, I asked, "Ken, how can you remember
so many?" "Oh, I've got a million of 'em," he
replied. Later he was acting dean after Orlo
Strunk accepted a position at Boston University.
In the summer of 1964 the Plummers visited us
again. They drove to a farm and bought lots of
ripe tomatoes and sweet corn. Then we had a
"Midwest dinner" consisting of nothing but all the
corn and tomatoes we could possible eat. Ken
wrote a history of Wesleyan College that was

published in 1965; that same year he transferred
to the History Department.

In February 1976 disaster struck. Ken took
a history class to visit a "hippy" commune near
Wheeling. He apparently caught flu and hepatitis,
and soon died. A memorial garden in his memory has been planted on the Wesleyan campus.

To return to our own lives, in the summer
of 1960 Gladys and I attended the Iota Sigma
Seminar and Consultative Conference held at
Springfield College in Massachusetts. As the
reader may recall, Henry Burton Sharman was the
compiler of the textbook of the course at
Willamette that aroused my curiosity about
Christian beginnings. For many years Sharman
conducted a seminar in a summer retreat based on
that book. In Sharman's last years a psychologist
or psychiatrist in Palo Alto was closely associated
with him in his work. Sharman made him executor of his will, which left funds to carry on
Sharman's mission. The Iota Sigma conference
was convened to determine how the funds should
be spent.

Some persons who had taken the course,
and especially those who had taken it directly
from Sharman and afterwards had taught it themselves, were invited. The conference was held at
Springfield College at the invitation of its president, Dr. Glenn Olds, who had taken the course at
Willamette. Thirty-two persons attended. The
twelve-day conference was a disappointment to
some of us because the executor and his friends
seemed determined that the remainder of
Sharman's funds should be used to foster a subjective psychological interpretation of the synoptic

gospels, ignoring their historical setting. That was not consistent with Sharman's own policy. This experience demonstrated the danger that a fund established by a will may be used after the donor's death for purposes incompatible with his wishes.

Three of my articles were published in 1960. A short note in the *Journal of Biblical Literature* criticized theologians for their tendency to be guided by their theological bias when they interpret the Bible. In the second article, "Qumran and the Fourth Gospel," I rejected the theory that the background of the Gospel of John is to be found with the Essenes, the Jewish sect at Qumran, and their Dead Sea scrolls. The theory was prevalent for a few years after the scrolls were found because a few parallels, or similarities, exist between them and the gospel. For example, a "spirit of truth" is in both, and both have a spiritual dualism. Their concepts of the spirit of truth are very different, however. Also, at Qumran the dualism is between a "spirit of truth" and a "spirit of error" (*Manual of Discipline* 4), but in John 3:6 the dualism is between flesh and spirit, an idea that was characteristic of Hellenistic mysticism and gnosticism, but foreign to the Essenes. The theology of the scrolls and the theology of the Gospel of John are *very* dissimilar. This article was printed in *Novum Testamentum*, an international journal of New Testament research, published by E. J. Brill in the Netherlands.

Two categories of Dead Sea scrolls were found at Qumran: canonical (i.e.., in the Bible) and those outside the canon. In "Qumran and the Old Testament," published in *Wesleyan Studies in Religion*, I discussed the significance of those scrolls which contain Old Testament books or fragments of them. Scholars were eager to learn what light these manuscripts might shed on the canon and text of the Old Testament, for they are the oldest biblical manuscripts that have been found. Was the canon at Qumran the same as the traditional Hebrew canon accepted today, or not? Did the Essenes at Qumran accept as Scripture the books of the Apocrypha, as the Jews at Alexandria did? I reported that apparently the canon at Qumran was the same as the traditional Hebrew canon, although the Essenes sometimes quoted from the Apocrypha, and they knew the Septuagint version of Scripture. As for text, the variant readings in these manuscripts indicate that several text-types were known at Qumran. Some of the variants, however, plainly arose from theological motivation; that is, some of the Essenes changed the text of the Old Testament to make it agree with, or support, their own theology. Later some early Christians used the same practice to support their own ideas.

Although we had many congenial friends in Buckhannon and we were happy in our work, Gladys and I did not want to spend the rest of our lives there. The isolation hindered visits between us and Gladys' relatives in Oregon, especially in the winter. The inaccessibility of research libraries was frustrating to me, for it rendered thorough historical research impossible except on out-of-state trips during vacations. Two geographical areas seemed to meet our need: Chicago and California. Chicago, especially, would solve my problem, for at that time the University of Chicago still had the policy that anyone who received a Ph.D. from that school could use its library free for the rest of his or her life, and in my field its libraries were second to none. California, especially Berkeley with the University of California and Pacific School of Religion (and Stanford not far away), would be an acceptable alternative, and would be closer to Gladys' relatives.

I renewed my registration with the placement office at the University of Chicago, but it listed only two positions in teaching religion, neither in my field of expertise. Gladys and I gave serious consideration to my switching fields and getting a master's degree in English or in library science. I sent inquiries to universities in Oregon and California, all in vain. In mid-February I discussed the matter frankly with Dean Strunk, who was not offended by my desire to leave. About the same time Gladys went to Oregon to visit her mother and scout for jobs for both of us in Oregon and California, but without success. By March 1 we had decided that I should not sign my contract for another year at Wesleyan, even though we had not found a position for either of us. When I told Dean Strunk, he commented, "That takes guts!" This period of uncertainty was a psychological strain on both of us; Gladys suffered pains in her shoulders, and I had pains in one leg. The cause was simply "nerves."

Gladys wrote to her former employer, the John Crerar Library in Chicago. The Librarian, Herman Henkle, replied, "Everyone around here who knows you would be most happy to have you come back at Crerar. As Walter Shelton [Gladys' former supervisor] says, 'Besides being nice to have around, you can do almost as much work as two other people.' Unfortunately, I cannot say right now whether I can find the money to hire even one of you."

Finally, Gladys received a definite offer from the Crerar Library, which she accepted in April. The die was cast; we would move to Chicago. We listed our home with a realtor and drove to Chicago where we signed a one-year lease on a large apartment on Kimbark Avenue, a few blocks from our former home on Woodlawn Avenue. Near the end of May we moved, and on June 1, 1961, Gladys began work at Crerar as the Serials Librarian, in charge of 13,000 scientific serials (publications scheduled to appear at intervals, either regularly or irregularly).

Teaching at Bexley Hall had introduced me to the lives of seminary students and had helped me to understand some of their problems. Their main religious problem seemed to be the contemporary tension between traditional theology and existentialist theology. Teaching at WVWC, however, gave me insight into the lives of undergraduates, whose problems were quite different from those of the graduate students. A few college students had difficulty in adjusting from fundamentalism to a historical view of the Bible and church history, but nearly all made the transition. The

atmosphere at the college was relaxed and congenial, and I fondly remember those days.   The
most valuable lesson for me was learning better
methods of conveying historical biblical interpretation to minds totally unfamiliar with it.

12

CHICAGO AND NORTHWESTERN UNIVERSITY

Housing in Chicago was still scarce. The apartment we rented was in bad condition, but the landlord promised orally to clean and repair it. Although his promise was not in writing, wherever we had lived a man's oral word was considered binding. After we had moved in, I reminded the landlord of his promise, but he said that he had not put it in writing and therefore "For you I fix nothing!" I complained to Chicago's building inspection department and to a neighborhood watchdog organization. The city department inspected the sewer leak in the basement, but did not enforce repair. The landlord was an immigrant from Europe who was determined to get rich quickly in America. His scheme was to buy as many old apartment houses in Chicago's Hyde Park neighborhood as he could, get all the money he could out of them without repairing anything, depreciate them as rapidly as posssible in his tax returns, and sell them a few years later at a large profit to the city's urban renewal project. The low federal tax on capital gains was a strong stimulus to such schemes. The landlord was reported to have become a millionaire from the tactic. The University of Chicago also bought surrounding buildings to restore or replace, providing another market for the landlord. We cleaned our dirty apartment, filled the cracks in the plaster, and repainted the rooms. When we moved out a year later, the landlord raised the rent to the new tenants because we had improved the place.

He owned the apartment house next door south of us, and used there the same trick of making false oral promises to lure tenants into signing a lease. One day I visited over the backyard fence with a tenant there, a black lady, and when I complained that the landlord had not kept his promises, she commented, "Iffen he do, it will be something new!" Her rhyme apparently was unintentional and the grammar imperfect, but truer words were never spoken. The experience opened our eyes to what many blacks in the North had to endure; they could not escape to better housing because none was available to them, and some landlords took advantage of the situation. As soon as our lease expired, we rented an apartment on Ridgeland Avenue for two years.

I hoped to establish in Chicago a business of producing and selling slide lectures on the history of religion, primarily for use by professors. My interest in Christian origins had grown to include interest in the Mediterranean religions contemporary with Christian beginnings because those other religions influenced early Christianity and its literature, including the New Testament. Gradually acquaintance with the literature and archaeology of those religions led me to broaden my interest to include knowledge of the history of religion as a whole. I had found from my teaching and from comments of professors who had used my slides that slides are an effective means of demonstrating conditions in ancient times. While at Wesleyan I had sold a few sets of slides, but the quality was inferior. I made the mistake of photographing black and white pictures with black and white film. When the lab followed standard practice and duplicated on color film, many weird colors resulted.

As soon as we were settled in Chicago, I produced new slide lectures on Greek New Testament manuscripts, using only color film. The text was printed by offset, on individual sheets, and Gladys and I slipped the sheets into printed covers and stapled them. Laying the lectures on the back of a plywood clipboard that my father had made, I flattened the staples by pounding them with a hammer. In my writing, for sentimental reasons, I still use that old clipboard, with its back deeply scored by the pounding. We kept the slides and lectures in an old trunk made around 1900; it was the first "office" of our slide lecture business. (If that isn't "cottage industry," what is?) The next year we put two more slide lectures on the academic market: "Ancient Tomb Paintings" and "Christian Catacomb Frescoes." Our advertising slogan was "Quality Visual Aids." In 1967 we added "They Searched for Truth," a slide lecture I wrote to call attention to fifteen pioneers who developed biblical scholarship. The two sets on New Testament manuscripts were very popular with professors and students, partly because they fit so well into an introduction to the New Testament, a course widely taught. At the end of six years, more than 250 schools were using them.   Although we had made a small profit, the market was too small to provide us with a living.

After we returned to Chicago in 1961, Gladys and I transferred our membership from First Methodist Church in Buckhannon to St. James Methodist Church in Chicago, where Jerry Walker was still the minister, as he was when we had joined in 1955. Again, we selected St. James because we wanted to support racial integration and we liked the sermons and excellent music. In 1955 about half the congregation was black because the neighborhood had recently changed from white to black. In 1961, the membership was more than three-fourths black. The black majority had changed the nature of the Sunday morning service, including calling out "Amen" and "Hallelujah" during the sermon. These new members from the South demonstrated the fact that when the membership suddenly changes to a majority from a different cultural background, the new members overwhelm the old by bringing in their former ideas and practices with them. The same process occurred frequently in the churches in the first and second centuries.

Two other members of St. James were Bismarck and Avery Williams, a wonderful black couple. Avery was a professional librarian, like Gladys; Bismarck taught economics at Roosevelt University in Chicago. We became close friends and socialized in each other's homes. A bond between us was that we all wanted to promote racial integration. A second bond was that we wanted to foster mature religion in the church. Bismarck taught an adult Sunday school class at

St. James and invited me to share with him the teaching function, which I gladly did.

In 1962 the Methodist bishop of the Chicago Conference replaced Jerry Walker with Harry Conner as minister of St. James. Harry was so conservative in theology that Gladys and I could not stand it, and we resigned from the church. I have another complaint against Harry too. He borrowed my copy of *The Conflict of Religions,* by Philip E. Ashby, professor of world religions at Princeton University. An excellent book, it describes the conflict in the major world religions between modern knowledge and old religious traditions. After keeping the book for months, Harry reported to me that he had lost it. I have been unable to replace it, for it has long been out of print.

As soon as I set foot on the campus again, I felt anew the allure of the University of Chicago, with its marvelous libraries. We attended some of the school's free public lectures, delivered by experts in their fields, just as we had done a decade earlier. In addition to other conferences, the university pioneered in the summer of 1961 by hosting a national conference for American Indians. I attended, and one of the Indians told me that this was the first time that all of the Indians had been recognized as equals with white men. Another Indian preached a sermon in Rockefeller Chapel on the campus. His theme was that Abraham's descendants were sojourners, or strangers, in a land not their own (Gen. 15:13), but the American Indians are strangers in their own land.

Chicago, I believe, matches New York as a crossroads of the world, for here many kinds of people meet and live. Many of the blacks and whites who had moved here to work during World War II chose to remain afterwards. Some Japanese Americans settled here after they were released from internment camps during the war. In 1962 my barber was from Greece, and our hardware merchant was from Turkey. Our neighbors in the apartment house included a nuclear scientist from Spain and an Irish-Catholic family from New Jersey. For years Chicago has had many ethnic neighborhoods which provide a wide variety of excellent restaurants. The University of Chicago has its famous International House where foreign students live under one roof, but the whole city is a home for internationals of all ages. Today many Hispanics, Orientals, and some emigrants from India add to the variety. Learning to know personally other races and nationalities fosters understanding and tolerance, if the environment is favorable.

We were greatly relieved when our house in Buckhannon sold in 1961. I planned to try again the next spring to obtain a teaching position in or near Chicago. Since I had taken undergraduate courses in philosophy, teaching philosophy and ethics along with religion might be a possibility for me in a small college. Therefore in the summer I took two graduate courses at the University of Chicago: one on Immanual Kant's philosophy and one on mathematical logic. Both were a waste of time; Kant's thought is obsolete, and the other course failed to make me think like a computer, the teacher's announced goal for the class.

In the autumn I began a research project, without a grant. In my research through the years I had recognized more and more the importance of knowing the Christian environment in order to understand the New Testament and the development of early Christianity. Many New Testament scholars have concentrated on studying the Jewish environment and have slighted the gentile and Christian environments. Therefore I spent twelve months reading and analyzing the early Christian writings outside the Bible. I asked myself these questions: What issues did the authors discuss? What problems in the churches were they trying to solve? I found enormous variation; different writers offered very different explanations or solutions to the same issue or problem. They even disagreed on doctrines. I recorded their views on each issue, typing them on filing cards. I had begun this project while I was at Bexley Hall. There I hired Allyn Walker to read carefully all of Justin Martyr's *Dialogue with Trypho the Jew* (ca. 150) and to put on separate cards exactly what Justin and Trypho had said on each issue they had debated. All the cards will furnish very important source material for my next book, *How Did Christianity Really Begin?*

An article by Sidney Temple[31] drew my attention to contemporary efforts to distinguish one or more sources in the Gospel of John. I was dissatisfied with the methods used by some biblical scholars, so I wrote a paper in which I tried to establish some valid guidelines, or criteria, for detecting source material. I read the paper at the annual meeting of the Society of Biblical Literature and Exegesis in December 1961; the paper was published the following year in the society's *Journal of Biblical Literature.*

Early in the spring of 1962 I registered again with several academic teacher-placement offices. Only one position in religion turned up, one at small Olivet College in Michigan. In my interview with the president it became apparent that we were far apart in our religious beliefs. He did not hire me, thank goodness; once again I was saved from taking the wrong path. But that spring I lay awake nights worrying about my future. "Was I crazy to have quit my position at Wesleyan?" I was fifty years old, out of a job, with practically no hope of obtaining a position teaching in my field. Nevertheless, the experience produced two beneficial results. It forced me to decide to become a librarian, and it made me sympathetic with people who are out of work--I know how they feel.

Having observed from Gladys' experience that library positions were plentiful compared with those in teaching religion, I reluctantly decided to become a librarian. In October Gladys was promoted to Head of the Catalog Department at Crerar, and in the same month I enrolled in the Graduate Library School (GLS) at the University of Chicago and received my M.A. in L.S. the following August.

While in library school I took a research course from Professor Howard Winger in which I produced sets of slides on old manuscript books, the history of printing, and early printers' marks. Just before I graduated the school notified me of a vacancy in the Order Department at Northwestern University Library.   David Jolly, Assistant Librarian, interviewed me, and Jens Nyholm, Head Librarian, hired me, beginning September 1963. I had to begin at the bottom of the ladder, with the same starting salary as any other inexperienced graduate fresh out of library school.

I had much to learn, for I had never worked in a library. In library school one acquires a comprehensive view of the field, and on the job one becomes expert in one's department. Some staff members who have worked for years in a library imagine that they know the field as well as those who have graduated from library school, but that is rarely true.   Both kinds of training are necessary if one is to qualify for administrative positions.

In the forenoons at Northwestern, with the aid of three assistants, I searched the card catalog to insure that we did not order books that the library already owned. In the afternoons I wrote letters for our department dealing with various problems, such as "We are returning this defective copy [some pages missing, or bound with cover up-side-down, etc.] to be replaced by a perfect copy." The Head of the Order Department was Vladimir Zernov, a White Russian married to an English woman. He was congenial and efficient, and I enjoyed working with him. One day I failed to detect that the library already had a copy of a very expensive book that Nyholm thought that the library should have, and I had a typist order it.   When it arrived, the Catalog

Department discovered that it was a duplicate of one we had. Mr. Nyholm scolded Vladimir, who took me out into a small garden beside the library and, in a friendly but firm manner, impressed upon me that I must never make such a mistake again! And I never did.

Olga Volkonsky, a woman born in Russia before the Russian Revolution, also worked in the Order Department. Unlike Vladimir, who was honest and ethical, Olga had a crafty disposition and was fond of playing sly tricks on people, especially Vladimir. One day a very important invoice disappeared, and half of the department's staff of ten spent twenty minutes turning the place up-side-down searching for it. Antonia Fodor, who was born in Hungary, suspected Olga, who was pretending to search for the invoice too. Finally Antonia concentrated on Olga's desk, and found the invoice under the large blotter pad on the top of the desk right where Olga had hidden it! Olga thought it was all great fun, but the rest of us took a dim view of it. Olga died two years later (No, we did not murder her!), and a few of us attended the funeral. That is the only time I have attended a service in a Russian Orthodox church.

As in many large libraries, the staff in the Order and Catalog Departments was quite cosmopolitan in composition. Northwestern's library acquired books and periodicals in many languages, and therefore some members of those departments needed to know those languages. My knowledge of foreign languages was a factor when I was hired; that type of knowledge is also useful in library reference work. One of the for-

eign-born in our department was Rita Djuricich
from Germany; her surname was not German because after coming to the United States she had
married Mladen Djuricich, an immigrant from
Yugoslavia. She checked in the serials and was
exceptionally fast and accurate in her work.

A man in another department was the an-
tithesis of Rita. He had a daily habit of touring
various departments of the library, during working hours, to visit with friends on the staff; he
walked fast, carrying a few books along, giving
the false impression that he was working hard.

Noel Owens, a Canadian, was Head of the
Reference Department. He was a scholar at heart,
and thoroughly enjoyed searching for the answers
to the difficult reference questions that faculty and
graduate students frequently brought. Noel
wanted me to work for him, and in 1965 I transferred to the Reference Department. Two years
later Noel persuaded the administration to create a
new position, Senior Assistant Reference
Librarian, and I was promoted to it.

Rolf Erickson, a recent graduate of the
University of Wisconsin's Library School, joined
our reference staff. Noel had placed me in charge
of the department's card catalog of its own books,
and I assigned to Rolf the task of filing new cards
in it. I taught him the necessity of complete accuracy in filing, and he taught me something too.
He observed that Noel had the habit of opening his
mail and then allowing the problems to pile up for
three or four weeks before dealing with them.
Rolf pointed out to me that it would be more efficient to solve the problems as soon as they arrived so that one would not have to spend time re-

freshing one's memory as to the nature of the problem. He taught me the rule: "Solve the problem now; don't postpone it."

Later I introduced Rolf to the practice of using one's spare time for scholarship. We compiled an annotated bibliography of books on changes in religion, but we never submitted it for publication. He had some old family letters written in Norwegian, consisting of correspondence between Norwegian immigrants in the United States and their relatives in Norway. Translating them aroused his interest in Norwegian-American history, a subject on which he is today a leading authority. Gladys and Rolf have Norwegian ancestry as a bond, and Rolf and I admire each other's thoroughness.

While I was working at Northwestern University I began to write book reviews. Professor Edmund Perry, in Northwestern's Department of the History and Literature of Religions, invited me to review books for the *Journal of the American Academy of Religion.* Later Judith Serebnik, the first Librarian of the Core Collection in Northwestern's new library, became book review editor of the *Library Journal,* and she invited me to review religious books for that journal. In addition, I occasionally reviewed books for the *Journal of Religion* and the *Journal of Biblical Literature*---a total of twenty in the 1960s and 1970s. The payment for this kind of work consists of a free copy of the book reviewed. Some of the books, however, are not worthy of a place in one's personal library, or other libraries either, and the reviewer feels that he has wasted his time. On the other hand, an author feels frustrated when the review is biased or inaccurate. The reviewer may not have read enough of the book to evaluate it properly. He may be prejudiced because the book does not agree with his own views, especially if he has written on the subject himself.

Professor Perry asked me if I would teach his introduction to the New Testament course in the spring quarter of 1966, while he took time off for personal research. I welcomed the invitation, for I enjoy teaching. I revised and updated my similar course taught at Wesleyan, but had to condense that nine-month course to three months at Northwestern.

When I was teaching at Bexley and Wesleyan, my summers were free for research, but I had only a little spare time for it during the rest of the year. The situation was the opposite when I was a librarian; then vacation lasted only three or four weeks, but during the working months my evenings and weekends were free. Wherever I was, I used my spare time for research on religion. While I was at Northwestern, I wrote a long article entitled "The Origin of the Son of Man Christology," which was published in the *Journal of Biblical Literature* in 1965. For the last hundred years biblical scholars have debated whether Jesus used the title Son of Man, whether it refers to him or to someone else, and whether the Son of Man in the synoptic gospels is divine or human. This subject will be discussed in my next book.

The next year I began a thorough effort to determine whether one writer or several produced the Gospel of John. The question is one of the most complex of New Testament problems, and certainly is the toughest I have ever tackled! Beginning with Jacob Eckermann in Germany in 1796, a multitude of New Testament scholars have observed disunity in John. The sharp breaks in thought, the variety of environments indicated, the inconsistency in the concepts of Jesus as the Christ, and the shifts in vocabulary, syntax, and style in the text in its original language, Greek-- all indicate the work of several writers. So much variation and inconsistency is characteristic of composite literature produced by several persons writing at different times and places; it is not characteristic of one individual writer.

Conservative Christians have always been upset by the suggestion that more than one writer may have been involved, for the theory is contrary to the old ecclesiastical tradition that the disciple John wrote the whole gospel. Therefore some of them have claimed that the book is a unity (in spite of the evidence), or they have asserted that the author must have written in a disjointed manner, perhaps at different periods of his life, or that he revised the book several times, radically changing his beliefs, vocabulary, and syntax between the stages of his writing. The theory that any one writer would make so *many* changes in his ideas and style and that he would not bother to harmonize *his own* writing--that *really* strains our credulity!

At first glance the question of authorship appears to be insignificant. What difference does it make? Why spend time on it? Actually, it has a major impact upon such matters as what Jesus did or did not say and do, why conflicting traditions about him arose, and what was going on in the churches when the gospels were written. The variety in the text is trying to tell us something. Are we listening?

I began my search by reading the investigations conducted by others, or if I could not obtain the original studies, summaries of them by scholars. In four years I examined all the scholarly works on the subject I could find, a total of 316. Some were in English, some in French, most in German. The main types of theories I found that tried to explain the evidence were that (1) the author, or evangelist, used a written source or sources; (2) a redactor, or editor, revised the gospel afterwards and added chapter 21; (3) the leaves of the original codex were accidentally displaced (that is, the codex came apart and someone replaced the leaves out of order). Displacement theories are no longer taken seriously, for they cannot explain the presence of conflicting ideas and the variations in vocabulary and syntax. During the first two years I hired a young man, Ray Cochran, to come to our home on weekends to type and organize my notes. He had a master's degree in journalism and had once started a newspaper in Buffalo, New York. He was a congenial friend and colleague. The next stages of my investigation were conducted after I transferred to Chicago State, and therefore they are summarized in the next chapter.

Because my job was in Evanston, at the north edge of Chicago, Gladys and I rented an apartment on the north side of Chicago in 1964, and in 1966 we purchased a new, large condominium apartment in Evanston, where we continue to live--the longest period that we have lived in the same place since we were married. Prior to 1966 we moved 12 times in 18 years.

Gladys' mother lived with us for a few months at a time in Chicago, Atlanta, Buckhannon, and Evanston. Between visits she lived at home in her apartment in Salem, Oregon. After we moved to the north side of Chicago, she came to live with us permanently, we hoped. We were always glad to have her with us, for she was helpful in many ways and with her sense of humor, fun to have in the household.

In her late years she had the misfortune of becoming nearly blind. She lost all sight in one eye and had only partial vision in the other. Because of our library jobs, Gladys and I could not take care of her during the day. Therefore in 1967 she flew back to Oregon accompanied by her granddaughter, Jean Windedahl, and for the rest of her life lived in a retirement home, Willamette Lutheran Homes, near Salem. This location was chosen because friends and her son and family lived in Salem, which had long been her home. Gladys flew out to visit her twice a year. Her mother died in the retirement home in 1970, at the age of 87, and was buried beside her husband in Belcrest Memorial Park, where my parents also are buried.

Mother-in-law tension between Gladys' mother and myself never existed. When I married Gladys, I feared that religion might be a problem in my relationship with her mother, but it never was. Although her mother held traditional Christian beliefs and I did not, she, like my own mother, was sensible and broad-minded by nature. Neither of us tried to convert the other to our own beliefs. Each recognized the other's sincerity and integrity, and we soon became quite fond of each other. Even after she lost most of her eyesight, she remained cheerful and congenial. She was a fine woman.

I resigned from Northwestern, effective April 15, 1969, to become Head of Reference and Assistant Professor of Library Science at Chicago State College. The Reference staff at Northwestern gave me a farewell party and a desk set, and I responded with an after-dinner type of speech, a wild account of an imaginary journey that some of us librarians took up the Amazon River to find manuscripts buried by Captain Kidd.

13

CHICAGO STATE

Some of my colleagues at Northwestern University Library thought that I was making a big mistake by leaving a prestigious university with a beautiful campus beside Lake Michigan, to work on Chicago's south side at Chicago State College, where the campus consisted of two old buildings surrounded by pavement. Another objection was that I would have to commute 25 miles to work, whereas I lived only a dozen blocks from NU. Nevertheless, the change made sense to me. At CSC I would have more authority and more salary and an opportunity to help students from low-income families. Those students needed guidance in using a library much more than the generally wealthy, better educated students at NU. At that time the CSC student body was 50% black, 40% white, and 10% Hispanic. In almost all cases they were the first in their family to earn a college degree. I wanted to help where I was needed most.

When I applied for the position in the CSC library, Dr. Fritz Veit was the library's Director. He was born in Emmendigen, Germany, just north of Freiburg, where his father was a grain and flour dealer. He studied in three German universities, receiving his doctorate in law in 1932 from the

university at Freiburg. When Hitler seized power a
year later. Dr. Veit recognized the danger for Jews
like himself if they remained in Germany.
Therefore he slipped across the nearby border into
France, where for two years he earned a living as a
tutor, teaching French to German emigres and
teaching German to native Frenchmen, His fears
concerning the Nazis were well founded, for later
his father and a sister perished in the Nazi persecu-
tions. In 1935 he migrated to the United States,
where he earned a Ph.D. in library science from the
University of Chicago. I found him to be a cheerful man in spite of the adversities he had endured.
A scholar, he had selected many important books
for CSC's library. I supported his work by developing the reference collection along Northwestern
University's standards. He was in charge of the
library at the West Center branch of the college in
Chicago as well as the library on the main campus,
and he taught in the Library School at Rosary
College.

I found that the Reference Department at
CSC had not been exerting itself much to help the
students; little personal guidance was given. After
setting an example, I trained my staff to give
prompt service and, whenever needed, show students how to find and use the proper reference
books and help them search until they found the
information if it was anywhere in the library. The
clerk-typist in our department had formed the habit
of wasting work-time by visiting over the telephone with friends in other offices on the campus.
She sensed that I did not approve, and after a few
months she transferred to an office outside the library. Having noticed my efforts to aid the stu-

dents, Mrs. Della Dunham, a black lady in the Catalog Department, asked Dr. Veit to transfer her to the vacant position. That was my lucky day! Soon two young white professional librarians joined our staff: Rochelle Sager and Stanley Schmidt. They, too, had a sense of mission to the students, and the four of us became an efficient team devoted to serving the students. Dr. Veit heartily approved.

For security reasons the periodicals, or magazines, both bound and current, were kept in stacks behind the reference desk. To service them and the reference books that were located at the desk, we had a staff of ten or twelve student aides, who worked in shifts. A problem soon arose. Under the former lax supervision the aides had become accustomed to loafing on the job. I called them to task, and there was a bit of a rebellion. Mrs. Dunham came to the rescue. Because most of the aides were black, like her, she asked me to make her their supervisor so that it would be clear that race was not a factor. This I did, and after she had a meeting with them, we had a fine group of industrious student aides.

Twice it has been my misfortune to be associated with schools at times when major controversies occurred. At Bexley Hall the controversy was between the dean and students. At Chicago State the trouble was between the school's president and some of its faculty. CSC was originally founded as Cook County Normal School in 1869 (the school was celebrating its centennial when I began to work for it). The Normal School soon became one of the nation's very best schools for training public school teachers and administrators.

Lacking necessary funds during the Great Depression, the school closed for a few years, then opened again in 1939. According to an account I read, the quality of the faculty quickly declined from excellent to mediocre during and after the Depression. Ownership of the school changed from Cook County to the City of Chicago (1909) to the State of Illinois (1965), and the school's name changed accordingly. The state enlarged the curriculum, converted the school into a general college, and began to upgrade the faculty. Around the time I joined the faculty (I did not teach; professional librarians have faculty status at Chicago State) the Illinois legislature voted to expand the college into a university, purchase land, and build a new campus. Dr. Milton Byrd became the president and supported the objectives of expansion and upgrading.

But there were still persons on the faculty who were judged to be unequal to the new standards. Some faculty members who feared that they might lose their jobs used the Cook County Teachers Union and the Faculty Senate to oppose President Byrd and prevent their dismissal. The union local called a strike when he did not renew the contracts of two of its members. I was shocked at the smear campaign and name-calling in the local union's propaganda in its weekly newsletter; such conduct was very unprofessional, and I would not want people who behave like that to be teachers of my children. The Faculty Senate approved or disapproved faculty promotions and tenure; this gave the clique in control of it a lot of influence. Opposing the school's president became the popular thing to do. Eventually the pressure was so strong that Dr. Byrd resigned. I was disgusted with the propaganda and tactics used against him and the abuse of tenure by some of the faculty.

While Dr. Byrd was still president, the State of Illinois bought a large tract of land in Chicago for the new campus. The land was owned by the Illinois Central Railroad and contained a round-house in the midst of native woods. It was the only large tract of land available in Chicago without homes on it. Thus the purchase had the advantage of not displacing anyone, and the school was welcomed by the adjoining black community. In 1971 Chicago State College became Chicago State University, and in November of that year it moved to the new campus, where many new problems awaited us.

The first problem was that we moved too soon, before construction of the buildings was completed. The state was paying rental to the city for use of the old campus, so it moved us as soon as possible and sooner than practical. I will never forget the first morning that I went to work on the new campus. The library building was surrounded by a mound of dirt ten feet high; that morning, after several days of rain, it was a mound of mud. As I climbed over it, I sank to my knees in the mud. The condition of the campus throughout that winter was reflected in the title of the daily newsletter the university printed: *The Mire Wire.*

Inside the library the construction crews got in our way and we in theirs. The bookshelves arrived from the factory three or four weeks after the move, and there was further delay while we waited for a crew to set them up. While we were waiting, the boxes of books were stacked all over the new library. At least all the reference books were stacked in the reference area. Stan Schmidt did a marvelous job of labeling the shelves in the old library and the corresponding shelves in the new library, adjusting the space in the latter to allow for future expansion. The movers, however, were inexperienced at moving libraries and stacked the boxes in random order. When someone wanted a book, we had to hunt for the box, which was liable to be at the bottom of a stack. When the shelves were finally installed, the movers returned to place the books on the shelves. Some of the crew had no idea that the order of books on a shelf is important--I doubt that they had ever used a library--and freely mixed up the books on the shelves. Afterwards all the professional librarians had to pitch in and straighten out the mess by "reading the shelves," that is, arranging the books strictly in the order of the call numbers on the spines.

Other problems consisted of some features of the architects' design. I had read an article in the *Library Journal* that reported that certain new libraries were having problems because the architects had ignored the librarians' requests. The architects were more interested in creating striking new designs than in planning functional library buildings. My suspicions had been aroused when Dr. Veit and I first met with a representative of the architectural firm. The young man had tried to soften us up by saying, "Some librarians have given my company a hard time, but I am sure we won't have any trouble with you." After the state had signed a contract with the architects to draft a set of plans for the whole campus, too much money had been invested for the state to shift to another firm. We had to settle, kicking and screaming, for whatever we could get.

One architectural mistake was the installation of a row of light bulbs, ten feet above the floor, around the two elevator shafts in the public area. The multitude of bulbs produced unnecessary light and heat. Our reference desk was beneath them and the heat was unbearable. At Dr. Veit's request the university had them all removed. Thus taxpayers' money was wasted on designing, purchasing, installing, and removing those lighting fixtures.

Two other architectural mistakes could not be remedied. The Order (or Acquisitions), Catalog, Circulation, and Reference Departments need ready access to the card catalog. At our new library, however, the Acquisitions and Catalog Departments are located far away from it, causing the staff to lose much time walking back and forth. (The problem was solved nicely when NU's new library was built, with the four departments surrounding the catalog.) Computerization of library catalogs can alleviate the problem. The other serious mistake, in my opinion, was locating the main floor of the library on the second floor, so that students and faculty have to climb many steps to use the library. Euphemistically naming the first two floors "ground floor" and "first floor", respectively, does not solve the problem! Students' and professors' time is valuable, and the heart of the library should be readily accessible.

The library on the new campus was named the Paul H. Douglas Library in honor of the Illinois senator, who was truly a great man, wise and car-ing. He participated in the dedication ceremonies, sitting in a wheelchair.

Meanwhile, Gladys retired from John Crerar Library at the end of 1972. She always had very cordial relations with both its administration and staff. She formed several lasting friendships, and she and her colleague in the Catalog Department, Mrs. Mabel Reynolds, continue to meet frequently for lunch together.

In the summer of 1973 Dr. Veit retired as Director of the library. He was a fair-minded colleague and had employed many blacks and Orientals without discriminating against them. I admired him for another reason also; he appreciated scholarship. He once remarked to me, "It takes a scholar to appreciate a scholar." At the banquet in his honor when he retired, I was privileged to give the speech in tribute.

Mrs. Minnie Johnson, Head of the branch library at West Center, now became Acting Director of the Douglas Library. She was offered the position of Director, but she did not accept it because she wanted to retire soon to care for her husband who was in poor health. She, too, was a congenial, fair-minded colleague. Born in Tennessee of black parents, Dr. (M.D.) and Mrs. Redmond, she remembered her father as a jolly man and her mother as a gentle lady. Mrs. Johnson, too, was a gentle lady. She graduated from Fisk University in Nashville and the library schools at Atlanta University and the University of Chicago. She became Assistant Librarian at Fisk and later the Head Librarian at Hampton Institute in Virginia.   After she had moved to Chicago, mutual friends induced Dr. Milton Johnson, a surgeon, to go with them to the home of "a friend" to pick up a book.   The "friend" turned out to be Minnie, and it must have been love at first sight, for a few months later Minnie and Milton were married.   I thought I was a fast operator when I courted Gladys, but Dr. Johnson moved even faster!   When Mrs. Johnson retired in 1974, I had the honor of giving the tribute speech at the banquet.   In appreciation of the librarians' expressions of affection, she gave them a Christmas party in December of that year.

On the new campus Annie Malone and Richard Higginbotham joined our staff of professional reference librarians; they, too, were a joy to work with.   We had a very good team, including the student aides.   Mrs. Della Dunham deserves special mention again.   Thanks to her industriousness on the job and continuing educational growth, she was promoted to academic rank.   While we were still on the old campus, she took evening courses and graduated from CSU, the first member of the library's non-professional staff to do so.   At the new campus she earned from CSU an M.S. in Ed., followed by an M.A. in Urban Studies from Loyola University in Chicago.   The library staff in general was composed of wonderful people, and I am glad that I had the experience of working with them.

The university's archives contained only a little material, so they were transferred to the Reference Department and I was asked to develop that collection.   In 1971 I produced an index of the actions of the Faculty Senate, using the minutes of its monthly meetings as the source. The index covered five and a half years, from the Senate's beginning in 1965. It was a big task, and I did half of it on my own time at home. The Senate gave me a vote of thanks, calling the work "a superb index."

In addition to its many programs for college students, CSU had a Gifted Center for gifted students of elementary school age. Its Director, Mrs. Dolores B. Johnson, and I cooperated regularly in giving these promising young pupils an introduction to the use of a library. They responded enthusiastically, and Mrs. Johnson was very appreciative of the Reference Department's contribution to the children's education.

I advanced in rank in the normal pattern. In 1972 I received tenure; in 1973, promotion to associate professor; in 1977 I retired as full professor emeritus at the age of 65.

CSU's annual Retirement and Recognition Dinner, held in June, was a fun occasion. After the university gave each of us six retirees a beautiful plaque in recognition of his or her service, the guests sang the traditional "Boo Hoo" song in which they pretended to be crying because we were leaving them! (Note: Everyone seems to have survived our departure.) Each retiree gave a brief speech. In mine I paid tribute to all in the university who were dedicated to advancing the students' education, with special mention of the library staff. Temporarily resorting to my after-dinner-speech style, I ended with a toast I composed for the occasion:

You have had many names;

You have seen many faces;
You've had many graduates
Who as leaders took their places.

You are becoming very old,
And alas, we are too!
But there's still life in us all!
So here's to you, CSU!

Some of my coworkers in the library felt that the library, too, should give me a retirement dinner, which it did on October 7 of that year. I was fond of the library staff, and the feeling was mutual. Their regard for me amounted "almost to love," remarked Allan DeGiulio, Vice President for Academic Affairs, on that occasion; the reasons, I believe, were my friendly and impartial treatment of the staff, black and white, and the special efforts to help the students. I still miss them all, staff and students. At the banquet the library staff gave me a five-volume set, *The Interpreter's Dictionary of the Bible,* an expensive gift which they knew I needed. In addition, the university's administration gave me a copy of Senator Paul H. Douglas's memoirs, *In the Fullness of Time.* This gift, too, was greatly appreciated, for it is a fine book by a great statesman, and I had worked in the library named in his honor.

Gladys and I were deeply grateful for this extra farewell banquet and gifts, and we responded by giving the library staff a Christmas luncheon in December. After the meal, I showed slides of our trip to Yugoslavia and Italy that year.

While at Chicago State I continued my biblical research in my spare time. The university gave me a small grant in 1971 for a research project and in 1975 a six-month sabbatical leave for additional research. Twice I shared some discoveries with faculty and students in the school's Open Forum series.

One problem in New Testament scholarship is the question of whether an authentic oral tradition of Jesus' actual teaching circulated among the churches. The question arose as a result of the discovery that the gospels were not written by the authors that tradition had ascribed to them. The authorship of the gospels is not stated in their text, but was assigned later in the manuscripts in the colophon added at the end of each gospel. This and other evidence raised doubts about the accuracy of the gospel traditions of the life of Jesus. If the gospels were not written by disciples who knew Jesus, then the next best thing, in the opinion of religious conservatives, was the theory that his disciples taught his words to their own followers, who memorized them and transmitted this oral tradition to others in their preaching. Some oral proclamations of the apostles did indeed circulate among the early churches, but did they consist of actual words of Jesus or were they apostolic preaching that originated in the churches?

I investigated this problem and found that the evidence is strongly against the theory that an authentic oral tradition of Jesus' teaching circulated among the churches (except his basic message in Mark 1:15): (1) When the apostles' preaching is described in the Bible, it is not presented as the teaching of Jesus during his earthly career.

According to Acts 2:22-36 Peter's preaching was not about Jesus' teaching, but about Jesus' crucifixion, resurrection, and ascension. In Acts 10:34-43 "the word" which the apostles preached to the people was the news about Jesus' baptism, healing, crucifixion, and resurrection; there is no mention of Jesus' teaching. Paul's preaching, too, in his letters, at least, does not report any teaching of Jesus before his death. (2) The teaching ascribed to Jesus in the canonical gospels is not ascribed to him in the other early Christian literature until after the middle of the second century, when the source is clearly our written gospels, not oral tradition. (3) The diversity of the "sayings of Jesus" in the gospels is remarkable if an authentic oral tradition was prevalent as the source. (4) Some sayings in the canonical gospels deal with issues that arose not in Jesus' lifetime, but in the churches after his crucifixion. These sayings simply cannot be the words of Jesus. On the basis of this evidence I read a paper at the annual meeting of the Society of Biblical Literature in 1969 in which I rejected the theory that an authentic oral tradition of Jesus' words circulated in the early churches. The paper was published in 1970 in the *Journal of Biblical Literature* under the title, "The Oral Tradition that Never Existed."

Professor David Aune invited me to write an article for a *Festschrift* (a collection of essays written in honor of someone) for our former professor at the University of Chicago, Allen P. Wikgren, upon his retirement. David was the editor, and the book was published in 1972 by E. J. Brill in the Netherlands. My article was a historical reconstruction of the beginnings of the early Christians' faith in the resurrection of Jesus. The next year *New Testament Studies,* a journal published by Cambridge University Press, printed my study of the use of the Greek article *ho,* which means "the," with proper names in the Greek text of the synoptic gospels. In a composite document the presence or absence of the article with proper names can serve as a clue for detecting the work of a particular writer if he did not use the article and the other writers did, or vice versa. This literary feature was useful in my research on the Gospel of John.

When I left Northwestern University, I had completed my survey of past scholarship on the question of the literary origin of the Gospel of John. During my first four years at Chicago State I conducted my own investigation. Using both the Greek text of the gospel and my own literal translation of it, and giving due consideration to the textual variants in the four oldest manuscripts of the Greek text, I searched for features that tend to occur together in some places in John. The features include ideas, syntax, and vocabulary. When certain features occur together in some passages and not in other passages, we have reason to believe that those features are characteristics of the work of a particular writer. Often in Greek there are two different ways of saying the same thing, and as a matter of style one writer chose one way and another writer chose the other. This often happens in John, which also contains sharp breaks in thought that indicate the later insertion of material into the gospel or into a source used in the gospel. The evidence is too abundant and too complex to describe here. After compiling a list of the characteristics of the various writers, I tried to identify the work of each one.

The basic conclusion that I reached was that John contains the work of four main writers. The evangelist, the author of the gospel, used two main written sources. One was the "Signs Source," or "Gospel of Signs," a narrative in which Jesus was portrayed as a human Jewish Messiah who performed miracles which the writer regarded as "signs," or evidence, that Jesus was Christ. The other source (probably a collection of documents, as Rudolf Bultmann suggested) consisted of a tract or tracts purporting to contain speeches of Jesus in which he revealed in a Hellenistic, semi-gnostic fashion that he was the divine "Son" of the Father (God), who sent him into this evil world in order that they who believe in him may have "life eternal." In the Prologue (1:1-18) the evangelist used a Christian gnostic hymn, which incorporated a non-gnostic Jewish poem. He inserted his own composition in many places in the body of the gospel and in the Prologue. Sometime after the gospel was written the fourth major writer, a redactor, revised the book, making a few insertions in it and adding chapter 21, in which he used three stories as sources.

The procedure and results of my investigation are presented in my book, *The Literary Origin of the Gospel of John.* The first half summarizes the studies made by others, and the second half reports my own research. I realize that the second half needs refining.

Rudolf Bultmann's pioneering work on the subject is incorporated in his commentary on the Gospel of John.[32] Later Professor Robert Fortna at Vassar College searched for the Signs Source in his book, *The Gospel of Signs*. 33 My conclusions turned out to be similar to, but not identical with, those of Bultmann, though I reached them independently. I disagree with his theories that the "Revelation-speeches" source, as he calls it, was originally written in Aramaic by John the Baptist's sect, and that the leaves of the codex were displaced and therefore the text should be rearranged. Bultmann, Fortna, and myself received much negative criticism when our books were published, but now an increasing number of biblical scholars are recognizing at least some of the composite nature of the gospel. Professor Helmut Koester at Harvard, in his recent *Introduction to the New Testament,* recognizes that there was a Signs Source.34 My Johannine research led to several papers I read at annual meetings of the Society of Biblical Literature.

   While still working at CSU I took the lead in founding the Religion and Ethics Institute.

14

RELIGION AND ETHICS INSTITUTE

On a sunny day in the summer of 1972 we were driving across southern Wisconsin en route to Carthage, South Dakota. Gladys and I were on our way to visit her relatives there and to attend a Carthage High School reunion. At that time I first suggested to her that we establish a nonprofit institute to promote modern knowledge of religion and ethics. The concept in my mind was still nebulous, however. I asked Gladys if she would be willing for us to commit ourselves to contribute $1,000 a year for five years to establish the institute; she readily agreed.

Several factors had convinced me of the need for such an institute. The more I had learned about biblical interpretation, the more fully I had realized that the churches were not teaching enough of what scholars know. Also, I had observed that the media were often negligent too. Most of the books, magazine articles, and newspaper reports pertaining to the Bible that are published either are in harmony with conservative Christian views or are unfounded sensationalism. A refreshing exception was the report on R. E. Friedman's book, *Who Wrote the Bible?* in *U.S.*

News & World Report in 1987.35 Once when I
was looking over the publishers' book exhibits at
an annual convention of the American Library
Association, I noticed a particularly worthless
book on the Bible. I asked the salesman representing the prominent publisher why his firm
published such stuff. He replied, "Oh, it sells! It
sells!" Another example occurred in the late
1950s when I attended an annual meeting of the
Society of Biblical Literature at Union
Theological Seminary in New York. The meetings of the society were rarely covered by the
press, but on that occasion a reporter for the *New
York Times* reported one paper that was read.
Which one did it report? The worst one! It was
the most sensational, unsupported by valid evidence.   Professor Geza Vermes at Oxford
University complains that the press in Britain
tends to shy away from printing "works of sound
scholarship in religion."36 Nevertheless, in modern times usually a few publishers have existed
somewhere who have had the courage and integrity to publish unorthodox works.

Radio and television programs, too, have
generally ignored biblical scholarship, and worst
of all are the radio and television stations con-
trolled by "Bible-believers," or "born-again
Christians." An inspiring exception is Chicago's
NBC station, WMAQ-TV, which for many years
has had three excellent religious programs each
Sunday morning: "Everyman" (Protestant),
"Friends" (Jewish), and "Gamut" (Catholic).
Formerly these three programs were telecast in
mid-forenoon, but now, if presented at all, are

shown when most of us are still asleep on Sunday morning.

After I acquired historical knowledge of Christian beginnings, I wanted to help make it known to the public. Later I aspired to do this also for accurate knowledge of religion in general. In the 1940s I dreamed that I would do it by writing books, but my first book was not even published. Through the years I saw that there were so many forces operating against the distribution of knowledge contrary to organized beliefs that the new knowledge did not have a fair chance in society. The idea of founding an institute as a step toward solving the problem was suggested to me by observation of various tax-exempt religious organizations. Conservative religious groups especially use this means of fostering their beliefs. Why not use it to promote religious knowledge based on scholarship? Observation at close range of a nonprofit organization, The International Greek New Testament Project, had given me the courage to think that I could manage a small nonprofit organization. I did not then foresee that Gladys would be an essential factor in the institute's success.

An attorney handled the legal work of establishing the institute. In order to file for a charter of incorporation from the State of Illinois, the Institute's name and a statement of its purpose must be in the application. I made both name and purpose broad in scope to cover anything the institute might ever want to do. This was important because to comply with the regulations of the Internal Revenue Service, a nonprofit organization must confine its activities to those consistent with its statement of purpose. For the name, I chose "Religion and Ethics Institute, Inc.," listing religion and ethics separately to make clear that both are included, even though I believe that true religion IS ethics and therefore the word "religion" automatically includes ethics. The statement of purpose reads: "to promote the discovery and distribution of sound historical and scientific knowledge in the fields of religion and ethics." Discovery and Distribution are the two Ds of intellectual progress in civilization.

Illinois law requires a minimum of three members on the board of directors of corporations; five seemed to be a reasonable number for us (nine at present). I am on the board, but I decline to hold office in it. Two close friends of mine who were also professors of religion were added: Horst Moehring at Brown University, who was a classmate when we were studying for our doctorates, and Harold Oliver at Boston University, who had been a colleague in the Project at Emory University. Professor Edmund Perry at Northwestern was a logical choice to broaden our base. An ordained Methodist minister, he had written his doctoral dissertation in the New Testament field; he was currently book review editor of the *Journal of the American Academy of Religion*. He taught Buddhism and had been an exchange professor to the University of Sri Lanka. I invited Professor Robert Grant at the University of Chicago, but he declined, saying that he was so busy that he was trying to get off boards and committees, not get on them. Next I invited Professor Wesley Teo, who taught philosophy and ethics at Chicago State University and thus represented the ethics field. He accepted, and the institute had a board of directors.

Illinois law requires that three persons sign the application for the state charter. Edmund Perry joined Gladys and me in signing as the three charter members; the informal ceremony took place on the rear steps outside his office. On November 29, 1972, the State of Illinois issued the charter. Soon we began calling the institute "REI." The lawyer furnished it with a set of by-laws which his secretary copied from a standard form for large corporations. It was too complex for our tiny organization, so I rewrote and simplified it.

The board held its first annual meeting in the Douglas Library at Chicago State University on July 16, 1973. Moehring and Oliver were unable to attend, but had sent in their proxies. Moehring was elected president, Oliver vice president, and Teo secretary of the board. The board appointed me as executive director of the institute.

The board decided to publish a series of occasional papers, beginning with *The Sangha of the Ti-Ratana* (The Order of the Three Gems), co-authored by Edmund F. Perry and Shanta Ratnayaka. Shanta Ratnayaka was Senior Lecturer of Buddhist Studies at the University of Sri Lanka. The paper, a scholarly study of the canon of Theravada Buddhism, demonstrated that originally Buddhist laymen were not regarded as spiritually inferior to monks, but had equal status; both groups, or orders, could realize spiritual *Nibbana,* Enlightenment. This differs from the attitude today among Buddhist masses, who regard the monks as holier than, and therefore superior to, the laymen.

At the same meeting the board voted to publish as REI's first book my manuscript, "The Literary Origin of the Gospel of John." When half of the manuscript was written, I had submitted it to Fortress Press, and the editor had expressed interest and asked me to submit the whole manuscript when it was completed. I did that, but the new editor returned it with the comment that the sales would not cover the costs, and that a university press might be interested. When I submitted it to Abingdon Press, I received a similar answer. Queries to two university presses brought negative responses. Then I telephoned Horst and asked if he thought REI should publish it. "That's not a bad idea," he replied. "After all, one of the reasons for establishing the institute is to deal with this kind of situation." The board approved. Gladys retyped the manuscript--except the bibliography and notes--ready for printing by photo-offset, and we published it as a quality paperback in January 1974. The customers have been professors and academic libraries in the United States, Canada, Europe, and a few in the Far East, Israel, and South America.

REI almost died at birth. Tax-exempt status (the organization is exempt from paying taxes) and tax-deductible status (contributions to the organization are deductible from donors' federal taxes), granted by the Internal Revenue Service (IRS), are essential for nonprofit organizations. IRS rules require that application for such status must be made within one year after incorporation.

Our attorney claimed that he had applied for us, but when the deadline was near, I checked with IRS and learned that he had not sent in an application. I filled out the form from IRS, just in time.

We soon found that we had another problem. The lawyer had not told me that to qualify with IRS, the institute must receive more than a third of its gross receipts from the public, not from the board or officers of the corporation. During its first year, however, REI's only income consisted of contributions from me, and I was both an officer and a board member. IRS saved the institute by granting it a one-year "advance ruling period," which gave us another year to receive enough funds (memberships, donations, sales of publications) from the public to meet the public-support test. We achieved the goal, and in March 1975 IRS officially notified REI that it had met the qualifications. IRS has always been fair with REI and very willing to explain the law.

IRS informed us that we must have members, so we sent out two bulk mailings to professors of Bible and Asian religions. The majority of the members who joined then were members of the Society of Biblical Literature, and REI has continued to maintain close relations with that society. In 1974 the institute began publishing the *REI Newsletter* (semiannually after that year), which is distributed to members of the institute. The newsletter has always consisted of two parts: news of the activities of the institute and a short article or bibliography on some aspect of religion or ethics. Members also receive a discount on the purchase of REI publications. Membership is open to everyone who agrees with the statement of purpose in the institute's charter. In the early years we gave one or two lectures per year to local members, but this practice was discontinued after 1980 because it consumed time needed for our main activities, research and publication.

After serving on the board for two years, Horst and Harry resigned because they were unable to attend board meetings. Several changes in board membership have occurred through the years, and the board has been broadened to include representatives of various professions and a variety of religious viewpoints. All board members must be, and are, dedicated to sound scholarship, based on objective research. The variety among the board members and their acceptance of the statement of purpose in REI's charter insure, we hope, sound scholarship by the institute.

An important development for REI was the decision to employ an assistant director. I had become acquainted with Paul Gehl when he worked part time in the Douglas Library while he studied for a Ph.D. in medieval studies at the University of Chicago. After graduation he spent a year at the American Academy at Rome. Then REI's board offered him the position for one year and he accepted. A financial risk was involved, however, for at the time the institute had on hand only a third of his salary. The immediate solution was a loan from Gladys, with the understanding that it would become a donation if REI could not repay. The eventual solution was part of the loan became a donation and Paul obtained grants for REI that enabled us to employ him half time for two more years. The only other staff member we have employed has been Rita Djuricich, who was a part-time secretary/clerk for several years. Gladys has been an unofficial unpaid secretary/clerk throughout the history of the institute.

I had given my slide lectures to REI for it to sell, and I had produced four for REI in a projected series of ten on the mystery religions of the Greek and Roman worlds. Paul obtained a grant from the National Endowment for the Humanities (NEH) to complete the series, and later got grants from it for a series of six slide lectures on the Old Testament in relation to its Near Eastern environment, and a series of six on Early Judaism. Our procedure was to contract with professors who were authorities on the subjects to write the lectures and to select the slides. We cooperated with them in making and acquiring slides and obtaining written permission to use them and any photographs reproduced. Upon NEH's recommendation we contracted with consultants, who also knew the subjects, to evaluate the slide lectures before we published them. REI has actively promoted and widely sold the slide lectures in the academic world.

When REI was founded I donated to it my general collection of 35mm. slides on the history of religion and ethics. Thereafter I steadily enlarged the collection by purchasing slides from museums, friends, and others, and by personally photographing significant items and places, with emphasis on archaeological sites and artifacts. Some friends donated slides to REI.

Gladys and I made eight trips to Europe together to add to REI's slide collection, photographing mainly in museums. The trips to

Scandinavia and Yugoslavia were mostly guided tours, but the other trips were planned in detail in advance and we traveled by rented automobile. Using an international directory of libraries and some travel guidebooks of the countries, we scheduled one or two archaeological sites or museums per day. Gladys recorded the photographs while I operated the camera. We also photographed in museums in the United States and Canada.

Our knowledge of French and German was very useful, and in Greece my knowledge of ancient Greek helped. We studied a little Italian, Spanish, and Serbo-Croatian before visiting the corresponding countries. The most difficult language problems occurred where there were regional differences within a country. In southern Belgium the language is French, but in Northern Belgium the language is Flemish and some museums do not have bilingual signs to identify the items. Asking directions in French in Alsace, I had no success until I realized that I was in a German-speaking pocket of France and I switched to German. Catalan is still the prevailing language in northeastern Spain, but the larger museums do have bilingual signs in Catalan and Spanish to identify the artifacts. Yugoslavia is very divided culturally and linguistically. One Yugoslavian told us that his mother becomes angry when watching television because the programs are in Serbo-Croatian but her language is Slovenian. We thought we would have no language problem in England, but when I asked directions from an English woman who was walking along the road just north of London, I could hardly understand a word she said!

Space here permits only a few remarks on our ventures, adventures, and misadventures abroad. The average condition of highways in England, Germany, and especially France was better than in the United States. The main driving problems were (a) finding a hotel, (b) find a place to park (parking partly on the sidewalk is permitted in most cities), and (c) finding one's way out of cities. Driving in some small towns on steep mountainsides was extremely difficult. The system at self-service gasoline stations in Germany was that when the customer stops pumping, a *Beleg,* or voucher, comes out of the side of the pump, and he or she must take the *Beleg* to the cashier.

One must beware of purse-snatchers and camera thieves in large cities, especially in areas frequented by tourists. Two of my cameras were stolen, one from our locked hotel room in Rome, and one that I forgot and left at the foot of the Acropolis in Athens for five minutes.

We had two narrow escapes in Barcelona. An English-speaking Spaniard watched us emerge from our hotel, and then followed us and claimed that he was a bartender there. He began to point out the sites while we were walking in the *Barrio Gotico* (Gothic Quarter, the old town). Soon he offered to take us into a cafe and treat us to a glass of wine apiece. When he persisted, we accepted the offer. Next he showed us a brochure which described various sight-seeing tours. When we expressed interest in one, he said the tickets were scarce, but he would telephone to learn if some were still available. He disappeared, then reappeared a few minutes later, saying he had reserved tickets for us.

"You pay me now. I get the tickets and bring to your hotel."

"No, you must first bring the tickets."

"No, I need your money to pay for them."

"No deal!"

He refused my offer to pay for the wine, but as we left the table he glared at me and said, "You break my heart!"

We did not get any free wine out of the other close call in Barcelona. As we were walking on the *Ramblas* (series of promenades) in a crowd, someone squirted a chocolate solution on our backs without our realizing it. Then a young man---an Oriental, not a native Spaniard--called our attention to it and beckoned to us to follow him to a nearby drinking fountain. Pulling a white cloth from his pocket, he offered to clean off the soil. Preparing to take off my soiled coat, I took my camera bag off my shoulder and started to put it down on the pavement. Then I remembered the warning, "Hold on to your bags," given to me by a desk clerk at our hotel, the *Colon* (Columbus), and I immediately put the bag back on my shoulder. The young man immediately lost interest in helping us and disappeared. We learned later that the system is for young thieves to work in teams of two, either two boys or a boy and a girl. After secretly splashing people's backs with a solution, one pretends to help the victims while the partner snatches purses and camera bags. Then both run and disappear in the crowd. One team told its victims that the soil came from pigeons flying overhead! An American woman living in Barcelona told us that a gypsy girl gave her a flower, and when the woman brought out her purse to pay her, the girl snatched it and ran. The same girl tried the same trick on her a week later.

The thieves and con men are not typical Europeans at all. Nearly everyone is friendly, eager to help, and honest. Waiters in France and Italy voluntarily gave back the extra money when I overpaid. When my billfold fell on the floor without my knowing it, a waiter in France picked it up and gave it to me. Another French waiter ran half a block to return a package we had left in the restaurant. On two occasions young men in Yugoslavia went out of their way to take us to museums we could not find, and refused a tip. Many people proudly told us they had relatives in the United States or had friends who had married Americans.

Our efforts to photograph in museums were generally successful at home and abroad. Occasionally a museum was closed when we visited it, closed for repairs or vacation, or because it was the closed day of the week. A few museums did not permit photography. Nearly all prohibited flash ("Blitz" in German) and tripods. A few charged a small camera fee. The best organized museum we found in any country, including the United States, was the National Archaeological Museum in Athens; its invaluable catalog is a detailed guide to its collection.

We often found significant archaeological artifacts that have not been adequately publicized. Let's take Mithraic remains as an example.

Mithraism was one of the mystery religions prevalent in the Roman world. Popular with Roman soldiers and traders, they spread the worship of the god Mithras from the Near East to Germany and England. Members were not allowed to reveal the cult's secret rituals, and therefore Mithraism is called a mystery religion. Excavation of their underground chapels is a major source of information. On our trips Gladys and I were alert for remains of mystery cults because of REI's production of slide lectures on those religions. Our trip to Germany and Austria in 1981 was especially successful in respect to Mithraism. In the *Stadtmuseum Noricum* in Linz, Austria, we saw a Mithraic bowl which probably was the common cup used for drinking wine in the Mithraic equivalent of the Christian Lord's Supper, or Eucharist. We drove east from Vienna to Bad Deutch-Altenburg near the Czechoslovakian and Hungarian border. The Carnuntum Museum there houses artifacts excavated at nearby Roman Carnuntum (now Petronell), where there was a Mithraic chapel. This museum contains a Mithraic baptism font similar in shape to some early Christian baptismal fonts. Later we saw a similar Mithraic baptismal font at Saalburg, near Frankfurt, Germany. Very few Americans know they exist.

Is Noah's ark on Mount Ararat? Sun Classic Pictures in Salt Lake City (later moved to Los Angeles) produced a pseudo-documentary film, "In Search of Noah's Ark," which tried to convince the public that the biblical flood story is true and that Noah's ark is on Mount Ararat. The

company rented theaters and, accompanied by a
lot of "hype," showed its sensational film in them.
The film attracted the attention of the National
Broadcasting Corporation, which purchased the
right to use it. NBC televised it nationally, in
prime time, May 2 and December 24, 1977. I
saw the Christmas eve showing and in behalf of
REI complained to NBC. I received no response,
so REI filed a formal complaint with the Federal
Communications Commission, with a copy to
NBC. NBC suddenly found the letter I had written to it. Our objection was that the film was
sectarian religious propaganda disguised as a factual documentary, using false evidence and drawing false conclusions. We objected to the misrep-
resentation of facts, the pretense of being objective, and the abuse of the documentary format.
We requested that NBC cease showing propaganda
films disguised as objective reports of objective
investigations and that it present nationwide, in
prime time like the film, the case against the his-
toricity of the story of Noah's ark and the existence of an ark on Mount Ararat. NBC's defence
was that the film was only entertainment and that
the showing was preceded by an advisory to that
effect. But some viewers tune in too late to see an
advisory, and others ignore it. Furthermore, the
film itself presented its contents not as entertainment but as facts proving that "the ark is there."
Afterwards I talked to many people who were
convinced by NBC's showing of the film that an
ark had actually been discovered on Mount
Ararat; they did not think that the film was
merely entertainment. Their experience demon-

strates the ineffectiveness of relying on "advisories."

The staff of FCC decided that "the program [the film] did not discuss a controversial issue of public importance [the legal requirements for FCC to take action], and no Commission action is warranted by your complaint." Actually, the real underlying issue was fundamentalists' interpretation of the Bible versus historical interpretation of it by historians, scientists, and major seminaries. If that isn't controversial, what is? And considering the widespread use of the Bible in society, the issue was certainly of public importance. I could have asked for a Review by the full Commission, but I did not because its staff had already decided against us.

Therefore I decided to fight back by writing a book on the subject. Working night and day, seven days a week, I wrote *The Noah's Ark Nonsense* in six months, and REI published it in 1978. Presenting the evidence, I pointed out that geologists and historians have demonstrated decisively that a flood over the whole earth has never occurred in the period of human habitation; therefore no Noah's ark is on Mount Ararat or anywhere else. In the same book I sketched the long history of the vain efforts to find "the ark." At the same time that I was writing, Professor Lloyd R. Bailey at Duke University wrote a paperback, *Where Is Noah's Ark?*, as a rebuttal to the film; it was published by the Methodist publisher, Abingdon Press. Not until we were finishing did we learn that we were both writing on the subject. Gary Wisby, a columnist for the *Chicago Sun-Times*, heard me lecture on the topic at the

Unitarian Church of Evanston, and he commented on my book in his syndicated column. As a result I was interviewed by 26 disk jockeys in the United States and Canada and by WGN-TV in Chicago.

In 1981 David Maloney, an REI member in Syracuse, New York, complained to us about the fundamentalist tracts that were being planted in the hospital where he worked. He suggested that I write a tract to counteract such propaganda. I wrote a leaflet, "When the Bible Becomes a God," which has been well received--except by fundamentalists!

In 1982 REI published my book, *The Historical Approach to the Bible.* Like my book on the Gospel of John, it was eight years in the making. The first half surveys the rise of historical interpretation of the Bible, and the second half describes briefly the main methods of the historical approach. As usual, I gave my manuscript first to Gladys for criticism. Next, my friends Paul Gehl, Arnold Nelson, and Richard Higginbotham read it with critical eyes. Our combined efforts resulted in a Certificate of Recognition in 1982 from The National Conference of Christians and Jews.

Although the institute's publications have reached many professors of religion and their students, they are generally unknown to the public. REI's books have not been sold in commercial bookstores, and the slide lecture format is not used much outside of academic classrooms. The institute would be more beneficial to society if it would find more direct ways of reaching the public. The growing use of video suggested to me that it could be a medium for distributing more widely the modern knowledge of religion and ethics.

At the Center for New Television in Chicago in 1983 I took an introductory course in video scriptwriting. REI's board of directors agreed that the video field was worth investigating and that our first video project should pertain to some aspect of historical interpretation of the Bible. Unfortunately for us, at that time NEH's Division of Educational Programs decided to stop giving grants for audiovisual teaching materials; educational video cassettes were included in this ban. We could hardly expect to receive a grant from anyone until we had demonstrated that we could produce video. Thus we would have to finance our first production ourselves from our own very limited resources.

I wrote a script for a 30-minute program on the history of conflicts over the Bible in Judaism and in Christianity, and engaged an inexperienced company to produce it. The result was so inferior technically that we discarded it. Next I persuaded the board to purchase our own equipment. Tom Hall set it up for us. With him as the producer and Jerry Bloom as the narrator, we produced a second edition of "Conflicts over the Bible." Although better than the first, it too was technically flawed. A defective camera added to the problem of our inexperience. We put the tape on the academic market, but still for a year I kept reshooting the slides shown in it to improve them. The next year, 1986, we produced "The Quest to Understand the Bible," two half-hour programs on the rise of modern biblical interpretation, based on my last book. Blake Beckstrom was our

producer for these. They, too, were not quite
perfect technically, but all three present important
information and pictures that are hard to find.
No other video or films give the perspective that
these provide. Having learned some lessons from
our first efforts, we are determined that our future productions will be of high quality throughout.

As I write this, REI stands on the threshold
of some new directions. The board of directors
has decided that the time has come to add the field
of ethics to our productions. In a few years
Gladys and I will have to turn over the operations
to younger hands. We are proud of the institute,
for it has made important contributions to education. We are grateful to its board and to its members, past and present, who have made the institute's achievements possible. REI has tremendous
potential for the future; it will continue to pioneer.

15

REFLECTIONS

My religious faith began as a believer in fundamentalism. I abandoned it when I learned some of its errors.

Fundamentalism as a movement began in the nineteenth century in Britain and America. The term "fundamentalism" is derived from a series of twelve booklets entitled *The Fundamentals* , published by two wealthy brothers, Lyman and Milton Stewart, in 1910-1915. They distributed three million copies. 37 Fundamentalists maintain that in order to be a Christian, a person must:

1. Believe that the whole Bible was verbally inspired by God's Holy Spirit and therefore the book is entirely infallible.

2. Believe that Jesus Christ is divine.

3. Believe that Jesus' death atones for the sins of Christians.

4. Believe in the Trinity. God consists of three persons: the Father, Son, and Holy Spirit.

5. Be born again of the Spirit [based on John 3; this is not the basis of salvation in the synoptic gospels or in the Apostles Creed].

6. Believe in Jesus' second coming.

7. Believe in Jesus' resurrection and ascension to heaven.

We observe that none of the seven requirements are ethical principles. Fundamentalists are so zealous for eternal salvation that they have been called people who are "hellbent for heaven." Their movement originated as a reaction against modern linguistic and historical interpretation of the Bible; they have aggressively denounced such interpretation as "Modernism" and "liberalism." They have always been extremely energetic in promoting their beliefs. In recent years they have endeavored shrewdly to capture control of some mainline denominations, particularly the Southern Baptist Convention and the Lutheran Church--Missouri Synod.

For the sake of clarity we should try to define "evangelical" and "mainline" churches, other terms often used today to classify Protestant Christians. Precise definition is virtually impossible because so much infiltration and crossbreeding has occurred among these groups since 1950.

Because the word fundamentalism has become, in the eyes of the public, virtually synonymous with ignorant, intolerant religion, some of that group disown the label and call themselves "evangelicals." The Statement of Faith of the National Association of Evangelicals is virtually the same as the "Fundamentals" of the fundamentalists, however.

When properly defined, "evangelical" does differ from "fundamentalist." Billy Graham has defined an evangelical as a person who (1) accepts Jesus Christ as his Savior and (2) accepts the Apostles' Creed.[38] Some evangelical Christians differ from fundamentalists in that they do not regard as necessary the beliefs in an inerrant Bible and Jesus' return nor do they insist on spiritual rebirth. "Conservative Christians" is an umbrella-label used to cover both groups. "Right wing" is often applied to persons who are ultra conservative in religion and politics.

The mainline Protestant churches include the Baptist, Christian (Disciples of Christ), Congregational, Episcopal, Methodist, and Presbyterian denominations. Often greater differences of belief occur within a denomination than between two denominations. Typically the beliefs of seminary professors are less traditional than those of the laymen, because the professors are more informed and understand the origin of some of the beliefs. Clergymen tend to be more liberal in theology when they graduate from seminary than they are ten years later, for they find it risky to try to change laymen's beliefs. Laymen may vary among themselves, for their beliefs are shaped partly by what they learn outside of church. Infiltration by conservatives in the last few decades has caused some mainline churches to lose their standards.

Undergraduate courses in Bible that I took at Willamette University awakened me to the realization that my fundamentalist beliefs were not fundamental, after all. In fact, they were not even true.

The fallacy of the belief in the infallibility of the Bible soon became apparent to me. Exaltation of the authority of the Bible began in the latter half of the sixteenth century, following the Reformation. In the controversy between Protestants and Roman Catholics, each group became dogmatic. Protestants used the Bible as their authority, and Catholics used the power of the pope and ecclesiastical councils as the authority for their position. The fundamentalist movement carried the exaltation of the Bible a step farther by making belief in the infallibility of every word in the book a prerequisite for eternal salvation. The Reformers believed that the Bible is the Word of God, but not in such a strict sense. Such devotion to the Bible has been called "bibliolatry," Bible worship.

Considering the contents of the Bible, it is incredible that some of its words and ideas were dictated by a perfect God. Some passages in the book are quite unworthy of a God who is love (1 John 4:8). For example, would a loving God command the Israelites to annihilate all their neighbors, as the Lord does in Deuteronomy 20:16-17?

> But in the cities of these peoples that the Lord
> your God gives you for an inheritance, you
> shall save alive nothing that breathes, but you
> shall utterly destroy them, the Hittites and the
> Amorites, the Canaanites and the Perizzites,
> the Hivites and the Jebusites, as the Lord your
> God has commanded.

Also, in spite of strenuous efforts to deny the fact, errors do exist in the Bible. For example, the earth is still believed to be flat ("the four corners of the earth," Isa. 1:12; Rev. 7:11). Part of the Old Testament quotation at the beginning of the Gospel of Mark is not from Isaiah as the passage states, but from Malachi 3:1. Inconsistencies and conflicting points of view occur too, not only between the Old and New Testaments, but also

within them.   For example, Paul states that
Christians are not obligated to obey the Jewish
Law now that Christ has come (Gal. 3 and 5), but
the author of the Gospel of Matthew stoutly
upholds every letter of it (Matt. 5:17-19).

Would a perfect God be so vengeful? Would
he, she, or it be so mistaken and inconsistent?
How can the Bible be the Word of God?
Although fundamentalists claim that belief in the
Bible's infallibility is absolutely essential for personal salvation, neither the Bible nor Jesus makes
such a claim. They do not even say that the Bible
is infallible. The Bible even reports Jesus as re-
jecting some passages in it. In Matthew 5:34 Jesus
disagrees with Numbers 30:2, which permits the
swearing of oaths; in verses 38-39 he rejects the
biblical law of retaliation, "an eye for an eye and
a tooth for a tooth" (Deut. 19:21).   In Mark
10:11-12 Jesus forbids divorce, which is contrary
to Deuteronomy 24:1, which permits it. When
confronted with such evidence, even though it is
in the Bible, fundamentalists invariably evade or
misinterpret it.

Giving the Bible so much authority produces
disastrous effects. It causes intense opposition to
historical interpretation of the book, for fundamentalists realize that the historical approach dis-
proves their assertion of the supreme authority of
the Bible. Omission and denunciation of historical interpretation causes widespread misunderstanding of the book. A second disastrous effect
of Bible worship is hostility to any scientific
knowledge that conflicts with the doctrine of biblical infallibility. Classic examples are fundamentalist opposition to the theory of evolution and to

geological, anthropological, and archaeological data that demonstrate that the earth and humanity arose gradually instead of in six days. Instead of accepting scientific evidence, those people put forth their ridiculous theory of creationism. Insistence that the Bible is the very Word of God is a severe hindrance to intellectual progress.

Fundamentalists also add to the misunderstanding of the Bible with their "prooftext" method of lifting verses out of context, ignoring what the author was really saying, in an effort to make the verses support their beliefs. A related tactic is to ignore or misinterpret passages which conflict with their views. These procedures are unfair to the Bible, for they do not allow the book to speak for itself.

The belief that final, authoritative religious words have been divinely revealed in the past makes believers afraid of new knowledge that might conflict with the revelation. Fundamentalists have combated such new knowledge zealously by all the means they could find, including:

1. Censorship of textbooks and libraries and the establishment of "Bible" schools and "Christian" schools to prevent young people from learning the new information. Organizations such as People For The American Way, American Library Association, and American Civil Liberties Union have been active in opposing their censorship. People For The American Way rightly emphasizes that children should have the "freedom to learn", they have a right to know.[39]

2. Creation of so much prejudice against the new information that people will not give it a fair

hearing. This is done by denouncing it as "secularism," "science," "elitism," "atheism," "communism,": and an "attack on the Bible."

3. Control of as much of the media as possible by owning and operating radio stations, television networks, and publishing houses to promote fundamentalist beliefs and to provide platforms for denouncing the new knowledge.

4. Use of every other possible means of promoting this concept of "mission." Tactics include distribution of tracts, correspondence courses, video tapes, and many, many devices to give their ideas a modern setting. I like to call the latter tactic "putting new dressing on the old rotten salad." Fundamentalists are quite ingenious at this. If they have left any stones unturned, I cannot imagine what they are.

Fear that new information may upset old beliefs is not confined to fundamentalists, however. A classic example is in the correspondence between Brooke Westcott and Fenton Hort. The men were Anglican clergymen at Cambridge University in the latter half of the nineteenth century. For thirty years they worked together, using the earliest manuscripts then available, and produced a Greek text of the New Testament that was closer to the original than any that had yet been printed. Early in the course of their work Westcott became fearful that they might weaken Christian faith in the divine revelation of the Bible. He wrote to Hort asking him to guarantee in advance that their investigations would not have that result. Hort replied that he could not continue to work with Westcott "if you make a decided conviction of the absolute infallibility of the

New Testament" a precondition for cooperation in the work.40 Westcott yielded, and the two friends completed the project. Intellectual progress in religion comes from Hort's integrity, not from Westcott's timidity.

A terrible consequence of the fear of knowledge is that ignorance in religion becomes a virtue, while knowledge becomes a sin. Religious leaders become blind leaders of the blind. European professors of religion are amazed at the fundamentalist phenomenon in the United States. And like some of the rest of us, they are dismayed that Ronald Reagan while president of this country publicly applauded it.

The fundamentalist movement stresses the belief that Jesus and the kingdom of God will come in the future. But according to Paul (1 Thess. 4:15-17), Jesus will return while Paul and some of his readers are still alive. In Mark 1:15 and 9:1 Jesus expects the kingdom of God to arrive in the lifetime of his listeners. These biblical passages are contrary to the belief that Jesus and the kingdom of God will come in the twentieth century or later.

When I read early Jewish and early Christian literature, both within and outside of the biblical canon, I was astonished at the tremendous variety of thought and practice in both religions. Each sect within Judaism had its own beliefs, and even those beliefs could vary within a sect. The Essenes at Qumran were certain they had the true faith and that all others, including all other Jews, were doomed. Divisions according to beliefs soon arose within Christianity too, and the actual religion of Jesus was soon set aside--a fact that conservative Christians are reluctant to admit. Those biblical scholars who have recognized major differences between the religion of Jesus and the teaching of the early churches are on the right track. In addition, both Judaism and Christianity have undergone further change since those days. The historical facts do not fit the claim of either Protestantism or Roman Catholicism that it has the original apostolic faith. None of the forms of Christianity today is identical with any form practiced in the first century.

After I learned the literary, linguistic, and historical methods of interpreting the Bible, I could see that their use is absolutely vital for understanding the Bible accurately. Those methods enable us to see what the writers were saying to the readers in their own times. The situations and modes of thought were quite different from ours, and some words had different meanings in those days.

I am glad I made an extensive study of the history of biblical interpretation, for it gave me perspective on religion as well as knowledge of the methods of interpretation. At a time when there is so much intellectual timidity and regression in religion, one finds comfort in the observation that, although the tide has ebbed and flowed, the long-range movement has been in the direction of more informed, more intelligent interpretation of the Bible. If biblical interpretation can become more intelligent, we hope that religion in general can also.

An interesting aspect of the history of biblical interpretation is that many of the reliable methods and essential source materials have been discovered since 1850. The earliest biblical manuscripts and many significant archaeological remains have been found in the twentieth century. In the same period the most advanced studies of the Bible and related ancient literature have been conducted. Thus this century has brought increased demand for change in religious beliefs, and laymen have had difficulty in adjusting to so much new information.

The biblical scholars and historians who have discovered valid methods of biblical interpretation deserve our praise. As a result of their intelligence, perseverance in research, and courage in making their findings known, we now have available a new understanding of the Bible, religion, and ancient history. Many scholars suffered by being denounced as heretics and/or losing their jobs. Along with philosophers and scientists they fostered an atmosphere of intellectual freedom unknown in ancient and medieval times.

While surveying the rise of the historical approach to the Bible, I observed that no valid method of interpretation was ever discovered by spiritual revelation. All were found by the hard work of uncovering facts and thinking intelligently about them--in short, they were discovered by scholarship.

Throughout history many persons have imagined that a divine spirit was speaking to them. This was often the case with Jewish, Christian, and pagan prophets. I never heard any divine voice, but I recall that when I was a teenager I often sang the hymn "In the Garden." It contains this line: "And he walks with me, and he talks with me, and he tells me I am his own." It was my favorite hymn. As I sang it meditatively, I actually thought that the Spirit of Jesus was with me. Later I realized that I had only imagined it. I am sure that imagination is a major factor in spiritual rebirth, or "born-again" experiences. A human weakness is our capacity to deceive ourselves.

I see no validity in "spiritual religion" that is claimed to be "beyond" and superior to psychological science and the physical world. Actually, all the spirit we know is part of the mind, which is the product of the functioning of the nerve cells in the physical brain. The belief that any spirit, human or divine, exists apart from the brain is a notion which lacks any valid evidence.

Study of the background of early Christianity gave me an awareness of the non-Christian contributions to Western culture that we have received from the ancient Near East, from Jews, Greeks, and Romans. Through Judaism we inherited indirectly from the Sumerians, Babylonians, Hittites, Canaanites, and Egyptians. Our heritage from Judaism, including ethics, is found not only in the Hebrew Scriptures, or Old Testament, but also in the Apocrypha, Jewish Pseudepigrapha, Dead Sea scrolls, and Mishnah; some of that heritage came to us through the early Jewish Christians. From the Greeks we inherited democracy, philosophy, ethics, art, and the beginnings of science. From the Romans we inherited law, government, and ethics. Later we received part of our cultural heritage from another source: In the Middle Ages Arabs contributed science, mathematics, and principles of grammar.

Americans often speak of "our Judeo-Christian culture" as though that were our only heritage. That is inaccurate and unfair, for we are indebted to many cultures. No man is an island, and neither is a culture. Religious conservatives often use "pagan" as a smear word, but that, too, is unfair. Paganism, like Judaism, Christianity, and other world religions, contained both desirable and undesirable features.

The traditional Christian theological beliefs do not provide an adequate foundation for religion in a modern world, for several reasons. Biblical/historical scholarship demonstrates that the beliefs were not really valid even in the first Christian century.[41] Second, those beliefs are quite unlike the religion of Jesus, which was quite unlike that of either the Apostles' Creed or the Gospel of John. Third, as history has demonstrated repeatedly, theological beliefs do not necessarily produce noble individuals or a "good society." In fact, wars have been fought over religious beliefs, and often both sides were wrong.

Religion in the future should be built upon a better foundation than either spiritualism or beliefs. Let us look at two old biblical ideals, "truth" and "righteousness," as alternatives.

Truth is an ideal in the Old Testament. "A righteous man hates falsehood" states Proverbs 13:5. "Lead me in your truth and teach me, for you are the God of my salvation," states Psalm 25:5. God is the "God of truth" in Isaiah 65:16. Knowledge of "God's truth" was a major goal of the Jewish sect at Qumran, according to the *Manual of Discipline* in the Dead Sea scrolls. In the New Testament, too, truth is associated with God and is exalted as an ideal. "God is spirit, and those who worship him must worship in spirit and truth" (John 4:24).

Admittedly, the biblical writers' concepts of truth were quite different from the modern scientific view of truth, partly because they lacked the knowledge we have, and partly because they had a very different idea of the way that truth is discovered. They believed that religious knowledge, or religious truth, is divinely bestowed by means of divine revelation. The idea that religious truth might be found by systematic investigation was utterly foreign to them. Spiritual revelation, however, has not proved to be a reliable source of knowledge, for the "revelations," even within the same religion and presumably from the same god, often disagree with each other. Also, the revelations to prophets, whether Jewish, Christian, or pagan, often contained factual errors. By their fruits we know them.

Increasingly the modern world has had to turn to more rational, more scientific methods of learning truth, including religious truth. Accurate understanding of the Bible has been achieved through the use of secular, historical methods, not through religious revelation. Christian doctors put their trust in medical science, not the Holy Spirit, as the source for determining what they should do to heal illness. Now many laymen and clergy rely mainly on secular psychology and psychiatry for counseling. The social sciences assist them in deciding what position and action to take on social issues. Academic research in seminaries and departments of religion in universities demonstrates the value of scientific search for truth in the field of religion.   At the annual joint convention of the American Academy of Religion and the Society of Biblical Literature professors publicly read research papers and criticize each other's evidence and conclusions. Although scholars may not necessarily regard truth as the basis of religion, they do regard it as very important. Otherwise they would not spend so much time searching for it.

Why not make the search for and acceptance of truth an essential ingredient of religion, even though it may temporarily be upsetting? The methods used to find truth should be reliable, consistent with or even identical with those used in scholarship and the sciences. In proclaiming what it perceives to be truth, religion should maintain an attitude of tolerance toward those who disagree, confident that eventually the truth will be accepted. Religion should also be willing to revise its description of truth in the light of sufficient evidence.

The second ingredient upon which religion could be founded is ethics. At the beginning of Christianity there was a general movement in the Mediterranean world toward a deepening concern for personal ethics. Stoic and Cynic philosophers, especially Epictetus and Marcus Aurelius, gave moral advice and maxims which are still worth reading.42 A similar concern is expressed in certain books of the Jewish Apocrypha, Pseudepigrapha, and Dead Sea scrolls. Unlike the Gospel of John, the synoptic gospels present Jesus as emphasizing ethics in his teaching. I compared the synoptic gospels' ethical teaching with that in

the contemporary Jewish literature, and I found
that nearly all the ethical principles in the synoptics were already in Judaism. In the synoptics a
man asks Jesus what he should do to inherit eternal life. The requirements in Jesus' reply are all
ethical commandments--not the "born-again" theology of John 3. "Love your neighbor as yourself" (from Lev. 19:18) is one of the Two
Commandments (Mark 12:31).

Regrettably, Christians soon were so involved
in theological disputes that ethics became sec-
ondary. When the Apostles' Creed and other
statements of what is essential for Christians were
formulated, no mention was made of ethical conduct. Although through the centuries ethics was
not discarded, priority was given to faith and
ritual.

Nevertheless, seeds of Christian social ethics
were sown in the Middle Ages. In 1025 Christian
heretics were tried by the Synod of Arras
"because they had asserted that the essence of religion is the performance of good works, and that
life should be supported by manual labour, and
that whoever puts these principles into practice
needs neither church nor sacrament."43 In 1221
lay followers of St. Francis of Assisi organized an
order known as the Tertiaries, which conducted
the social work of the Franciscan Order. The
Tertiaries condemned the Church and the papacy
for their love of wealth. Many of the heretical
sects of the Middle Ages were poor and denounced the Church for its worldliness, which
contrasted sharply with their own poverty. The
most famous of these sects was the group of itin-
erant preachers (both women and men) founded

by John Wycliffe around 1400; the Lollards, as they were called, preached from Wycliffe's English translation of the Bible. They were concerned with personal morality as well as economic justice. Later a Christian socialist movement arose among the poor which protested the wealth of the capitalist class. For five centuries (1500-1900) many Christian movements appeared and disappeared that advocated social and economic justice, including Christian communism and Christian socialism.44 Christian personal ethics were presented from a very pietistic point of view in two classic books, *Imitation of Christ* (15th c.), ascribed to Thomas a Kempis, and *Pilgrim's Progress*, by John Bunyan (17th c.).

In the nineteenth century the German Protestant professor, Albrecht Ritschl, rejected mysticism as the basis of religion, and replaced it with the ideal of the kingdom of God on earth in which universal love of neighbor would prevail. Adolf von Harnack and a number of other German Protestant theologians developed his view. The idea soon spread to England and America. In America the kingdom of God movement was called "the Social Gospel"; it reached its peak early in the twentieth century.

The leading exponent of the Social Gospel was Walter Rauschenbusch. The first eleven years of his career were spent in New York City as minister of a small Baptist church adjacent to a slum district. Acquaintance with the depressed economic conditions of his parishioners convinced him that traditional theology is inadequate to meet the needs of the people. In 1897 he became professor of church history at the Rochester

Theological Seminary. While there he wrote several books, including his famous *A Theology for the Social Gospel*. He maintained that the purpose of the Christian religion is to build the kingdom of God on earth; he cited as evidence the beginning of the Lord's Prayer: "Thy kingdom come; thy will be done on earth." Some other leaders followed him, and the Social Gospel was very popular for two decades, but it faded with World War I, which made it seem hopeless, and the prosperity of the 1920s made it seem unnecessary. Further, biblical scholars pointed out that its foundation was a misinterpretation of the kingdom of God that Jesus preached. Contrary to the tenets of the Social Gospel, Jesus did not free the concept of the kingdom of God from Jewish nationalism and the belief that the kingdom was coming suddenly and supernaturally in his day. Jesus did not expect Christians to build the kingdom gradually in the twentieth century or any other.

A current theology which combines Christian faith with social ethics is "liberation theology." Its goal is to liberate mankind from sin and oppression of all kinds, including poverty, illiteracy, and deprivation of human rights. It seeks to minister to both "body and soul." It emerged from Vatican Council II in the 1960s and was later espoused by the World Council of Churches.

I have sketched some highlights of the history of Christian ethics in order to demonstrate that the idea of ethics as a foundation of religion is not too foreign to the Christian faith. Neither is the idea utterly foreign to Judaism with its strong emphasis on the necessity of doing good works. I am not listing brotherly love, or goodwill toward mankind, as a separate basic because I regard it as an essential ingredient of ethics.

Throughout history humanity has found that both truth and ethics are essential in the secular realm too. When truth and honesty did not prevail in family relations, in commerce, or in covenants or treaties between tribes and nations, trouble resulted. When a man murdered his neighbor or stole his property, the consequences were so undesirable that laws were made to punish the guilty and to try to prevent future occurrences. The actual source of the Ten Commandments was not divine revelation at Mount Sinai, but the secular experiences of the people. The laws were given authority by ascribing them to "the Lord," even as the Babylonian king Hammurabi gave his legal decrees authority by ascribing them to the sun god Shamash. Experience has long demonstrated the importance of truth and ethics in human relations.

If truth and ethics are to be the foundation of religion, how should those terms be defined? Truth consists of ideas and beliefs based on accurate factual information as interpreted by sound logic, or reason. Ethics consists of personal and social attitudes and actions that promote the welfare of the individual and society as a whole.

The need for truth and ethics in today's world is so obvious that it hardly need be argued here. Politics and conservative religion have crucified both truth and ethics. Unethical treatment of peoples causes national and international conflicts. Greed and corruption have permeated society;

drugs, crime, and lack of ethical standards are tearing it apart.

People tend to think that ethics are nice to have, but are not really practical. Until recently students who studied ethics were very rare, and of them, fewer still thought of ethics as essential for their careers or the development of society. Actually, many of the world's problems would be solved if everyone practiced fairness, tolerance, and honesty. Although some individuals succeed by unethical means, their success may be only temporary and may spoil their personality and peace of mind. The more I see of life, the more I am convinced of the practicality of ethics for both the individual and society.

In the last two decades conservative Protestantism has grown rapidly in the United States, but at the same time morality has declined. The situation suggests (as a Gallup poll indicated 45) that churches do not have as much influence on the conduct of their members as they did formerly. Wouldn't the churches' ethical teachings be taken more seriously if they were not associated with theological beliefs we do not *really* believe?

Will existing religions rise to the need? The outlook is dim. Declining membership, lack of initiative, and conservative influence render mainline Protestantism too weak to be very effective. Conservative Protestantism is not even interested in the truthful understanding of religion. Roman Catholicism is weakened by its autocratic policy and papal resistance to theological liberalism, contraception, and abortion. (The best features of Catholicism today are its genuine concern for the world's underprivileged and the contributions to biblical scholarship of some professors.) Orthodox and Conservative Judaism are tied to ethnic traditions. Reform Judaism has advanced toward truth and ethics, but its ethnic background prevents it from appealing to non-Jews as a universal religion.

The Unitarian Universalist Association is a liberal denomination which is more open to change than Judaism and Christianity. Although there have been Unitarian churches in America since 1796, the denomination is still small. The reasons for its slow growth, in my opinion, are its diversity of thought, the diffusion of its funds to charitable causes when other churches were giving priority to self-promotion, and the rejection of rewards in heaven as a lure for membership. More than any other church, it recognizes truth and ethics as the essence of religion. Nevertheless, its emphasis on freedom of thought in the church prevents it from uniting behind a detailed religious philosophy and from developing a concrete program to promote it.

I would like to see some institution, either extant or yet to be organized, use research to formulate a detailed philosophy of religion with truth and ethics as the foundation stones. After accomplishing that goal, it should produce the programs and materials for use in the exercise and promotion of that religion. The religion should incorporate whatever is necessary to give its members the knowledge and inspiration essential for the intelligent conduct of personal and social ethics in an atmosphere of brotherhood.

This religion would not be shackled to the traditions of the past. Its appeal would not be racial, ethnic, or national, but universal. It should be organized with its own churches, with central administrative headquarters, and a research center to guide and develop its programs. The programs should include scientific and cultural knowledge essential for living a constructive personal life with concern for the welfare of humanity throughout the world, present and future. The growth of personal and social ethics should be aggressively sought. The programs should also include an accurate understanding of ethics, psychology, sociology, personality development, history, philosophy, and religions, including the Bible and the history of its interpretation. Some of its ritual, especially its songs, should stimulate inspirational emotion consistent with facts and reason.

A religion of this type has never been developed.

Appendix

ORIGIN OF THE NAME "TEEPLE"

The name Teeple is apparently an Americanization of the German family name "Diebel." In 1984 The Genealogical Society published mirofiche which report genealogical evidence from many countries. I examined them and found no "Teeple" before 1800. The name in the microfiche that is the closest is that of Adam Teepel, whose daughter Caroline was christened in Prussia in 1818; perhaps Adam or an ancestor of his was an American who returned to Germany. I would like to know if there were any "Teeple" names in German lands before 1700.

In tracing family names we must realize that the names of many European immigrants were Americanized, especially along phonetic lines. Colonial officials and others recorded the names the way they sounded to them, and immigrants changed the spelling accordingly. In changing German names to American spelling, d was often changed to t, and b to p. Also, ie, which in German is pronounced "ee," could naturally be changed to ee in English spelling. Thus the change from "Diebel" to "Teeple" is not at all surprising. Phonetic changes in spelling occurred in Germany too, however. For example,

Deutschland is spelled *"Teutschland"* in the title of Simmendinger's pamphlet (published 1717) which lists the names of some Palatinate emigrants.

The Genealogical Society's microfiche list several dozen persons living in Hesse, Prussia, and Bavaria in the eighteenth and nineteenth centuries with the names Deibel, Deibbel, or Deibels. None of those forms are probable as the antecedent of the name Teeple because the pronunciation of ei in German is like English "eye," and Deibel would not sound like Teeple.

Filby's *Index (1982-85 Cumulation,* p. 704) of ship passenger and immigration lists reports a "Peter Diebel" who migrated to New Jersey in 1709 with wife and three children. He was not an ancestor of mine, but he confirms that the name Diebel existed among the early German immigrants. The Dutch embarkation list of passengers who sailed from Rotterdam to England on July 28, 1709, en route to America include a "Johan Peter Diepel" with wife and three children. If the two Peters are the same man, we have here an early stage in the transition from "Diebel" to "Teeple."

The name Diebel is pronounced "Deeble" in German. We have evidence that was the pronunciation of the name of my ancestor Hans George Teeple. The records of the Lutheran Church in New York City in 1739 recorded his name (when he married the third time) as "Hans George Debele" (Chambers, *Early Germans in New Jersey,* p. 525). In Americanized English Debele was pronounced the same as Diebel in German, and the church simply wrote the name as it sounded to the recorder's ears.

Sometimes consonants in family names were doubled when a name was transmitted. For example, the family name of Elizabeth Diebel (married in Hesse in 1756) was changed to "Tibbel" (Genealogical Society microfiche, "Hesse, Diebel").

Clear evidence of the transformation of "Diebel" to "Teeple" occurs in the will of George Lucas Teeple, who was the son of William, who was the brother of my ancestor, Hans George. Lucas, as he was called, was born in Germany in 1698 and emigrated as a child. On August 20, 1774, he made his will in Somerset County, New Jersey, at the age of 76, and signed his name on it as "Lucas Diebble." His son Christopher, as coexecutor of the will, signed his own name as "Christopher Dipple." The attorney or whoever wrote the will spelled the surname of both men as "Teeple." My wife and I examined a copy of the will on microfilm in the Archives Room of the New Jersey State Library in Trenton. We were astonished to find three different spellings of the family name in one legal document--even father and son spelled it differently! A librarian at the desk told us that variant spellings, even in the same document, often occurred in colonial America. My friend Fritz Veit, who grew up in Germany, has told me that in those days the spelling of family names changed freely in Germany too. I have been told that there are still families with the name Diebel living in the Black Forest region of Germany.

NOTES

1. The first synopsis in English of the synoptic gospels was *A Harmonie upon the three Evangelists, Matthew, Mark, and Luke*, published in 1584 in London. Many have been published since, including Burton H. Throckmorton, Jr., *Gospel Parallels* (4th ed., New York, 1979), which is a synopsis of the RSV translation of the synoptics. An early synopsis of the Greek text of the synoptic gospels was Johann Griesbach's published in 1776. Kurt Aland in Germany produced a synopsis of the Greek text of all four canonical gospels, *Synopsis Quattuor Evangelium* (Stuttgart, 1964). Recently Robert W. Funk compiled *New Gospel Parallels* (2 vols., Philadelphia, 1985) which includes parallels from apocryphal gospels. John D. Crossan's *Sayings Parallels* (Philadelphia, 1986) is a compilation from early Christian literature of sayings attributed to Jesus.

A synopsis should be distinguished from a harmony, which is an effort to blend the four canonical gospels into one harmonious account. That task is impossible, for there is so much variation among the gospels, especially between John and the other three. The 1584 *Harmonie* mentioned above was really a synopsis, not a harmony.

2. For information about Teeple ancestors I am particularly indebted to E. A. Owen, *Pioneer Sketches of Long Point Settlement* (Toronto, 1898), and Lorne E. Teeple, "The Teeple People" (unpub. ms., Arkona, Ontario, 1984). See also the *Index* to Owens' book, published by the Norfolk Historical Society (Simcoe, Ont., 1980). Wm. Lloyd Teeple in Woodstock, Ontario, was very helpful.

3. See "Appendix" in this book.

4. See John O. Evjen, *Scandinavian Immigrants in New York: 1630-1674* (Minneapolis, 1916), Appendix IV, "German Immigrants in New York, 1630-1674." See also Lucy F. Bittinger, *The Germans in Colonial Times* (Philadelphia, 1901); Henry E. Jacobs, *The German Emigration to America: 1709-1740* (Lancaster, Pa., 1898). According to the German Genealogical Society in America, the first *organized* group of German immigrants to the New World arrived in Philadelphia October 6, 1683 (Nat. Gen. Soc. *Bulletin*, Summer, 1987).

5. James P. Snell, *History of Hunterdon and Somerset Counties, New Jersey,* 2 vols. (Philadelphia, 1881), 2:559.

6. A Margaret Teiple bought a propriety in undivided land in Eastern New Jersey from Alexander McDowell in 1727. Was she the sister of the three Teeple brothers or not?

7. Theodore F. Chambers, *The Early Germans in New Jersey* (Dover, N.J., 1895), 525.

8. The recorded deed is on microfilm "Somerset 6" in the Archives Room of the New Jersey State Library.

9.   A. Van Doren Honeyman, ed., *Northwestern New Jersey* (New York, 1927), 1:36.

10. Chambers, loc. cit.

11. Andrew D. Mellick, Jr., *The Story of an Old Farm or Life in New Jersey in the Eighteenth Century* (Somerville, N.J., 1889), 93-94. On the site of St. Paul's Lutheran Church, which burned down, a Methodist church was erected in 1831. After the Methodist church was moved in 1850, a schoolhouse was built there (Honeyman, op. cit., 297). Pluckemin's police station now stands on the site, I was told. The earliest church at Pluckemin was a Dutch church established in 1721. The Zion Lutheran Church in New Germantown (now Oldwick) was erected in 1750 and still stands, in remodeled form.

12. Chambers, op. cit., 288-89.

13. Mellick, op. cit., 164.

14. Ibid., 93-94.

15.   Chambers, op. cit., 525; *The Genealogical Magazine of New Jersey,* 31 (1956):15.

16. Mellick, op. cit., 430.

17. E. A. Owen, *Pioneer Sketches of Long Point Settlement,* 131.

18. Ibid., 38.

19. Ibid., 37.

20. W. B. Waterbury, "The Teeple Family Record: 1762-1899" (unpublished ms.; St. Thomas, Ont., 1899).

21. Owen, op. cit., 468.

22. For history of the pioneer town, see Bruce Ramsey, *Five Corners: The Story of Chilliwhack* (Chilliwack, B.C., 1975).

23. *The Noah's Ark Nonsense* (Evanston, Ill., 1978).

24. Two of Gladys' relatives, Hallvard Natvik in Volda, Norway, and Jarl Natwick in Morristown, Tenn., have recently compiled genealogical/biographical books which were helpful in tracing her paternal relatives in the mid-nineteenth century. Jarl's surname illustrates the fact that in the United States the spelling was changed to Natwick. The migration of Gladys' maternal great-grandparents Larsgard and children is briefly reported in a book written in Norwegian by Lars and Sigurd Reinton *(Folk og Fortid i Hol* ["People and Past in Hol"], II (Oslo, 1969), 2:747, entry "Ola Embrikkson Larsgard").

25. A homestead was a tract of 160 acres (a quarter section) acquired from U.S. public lands by filing a record and living on and cultivating the tract for five years. A preemption was the right or option, given by the Federal government to the settler on a tract of U. S. public land, to have the first right to purchase the tract. A tree claim entitled a settler to an additional 160 acres provided he planted some trees on it.

26. Cited from its *History of Clayton County,* 116.

27. Reinton and Reinton, op. cit., 614.

28. William Hedgepeth, "Koinonia," *Intellectual Digest,* Nov. 1971, 64. See also William Hedgepeth, *The Alternative: Communal Life in New America* (New York, 1970).

29. For a history of the Project see J. K. Elliott, "The International Project to Establish a Critical Apparatus to Luke's Gospel," *New*

Testament Studies 29 (1983): 531-38. For an account of its beginnings, see Merrill M. Parvis, "The International Project to Establish a New Critical Apparatus of the Greek New Testament," *Crozer Quarterly* 27 (1950) :301-8.

30. International Greek New Testament Project, *The Gospel according to St. Luke,* 2 vols., The New Testament in Greek Series, 3 (Oxford, 1984-87).

31. Sidney Temple, "A Key to the Composition of the Fourth Gospel," *Journal of Biblical Literature* 80 (1961) :220-32.

32. Rudolf Bultmann, *The Gospel of John: A Commentary* (Philadelphia, 1971), tr. from the 1964 German edition. Bultmann was Professor of New Testament at Marburg University in West Germany.

33. Robert T. Fortna, *The Gospel of Signs,* Society for New Testament Studies Monograph Series, 11 (Cambridge, 1970).

34. Helmut Koester, *Introduction to the New Testament,* 2 vols. (Berlin and New York, 1982).

35. August 24, 1987, 52-53. *Time* magazine printed a fairly good report on scholarship on Jesus ("Who Was Jesus?,"Aug. 15, 1988).

36. Geza Vermes, *Jesus and the World of Judaism* (Philadelphia, 1984), 145, n. 4.

37. Ernest R. Sandeen, *The Roots of Fundamentalism* (Chicago, 1970), chap. 8.

38. Billy Graham, on Jorie Luloff's TV program on Channel 5, Chicago, Sept. 1980.

39. See Edward B. Jenkinson, *Censors in the Classroom: The Mind Benders* (Carbondale,

Ill., 1979;); Barbara Parker and Stefanie Weiss, *Protecting the Freedom to Learn: A Citizen's Guide* (Washington, D.C., 1983).

40.   Cited from Stephen Neill, *The Interpretation of the New Testament: 1861-1961* (New York, 1964), 89, n. 2.

41. I will discuss the origin of those beliefs in my book on the beginning of Christianity.

42.   Epictetus' *Discourses* and Marcus Aurelius' *Meditations* are readily available. For Cynic writings, see Abraham J. Malherbe, *The Cynic Epistles,* published by Scholars Press (now in Atlanta), 1977.

43.   William Dale Morris, *The Christian Origins of Social Revolt* (London, 1949), 12-13.

44.   For a fascinating account, read Morris, op. cit.

45.   Cited from *Emerging Trends* in an undated letter (soliciting subscriptions) signed by George Gallup, Jr.

P. 1